The
Problem
Solver

MONTSERRAT
PRESS

Friends of *The Problem Solver*

"I love how *The Problem Solver* portrays life. We get to choose. Do we want to solve our problems with our own strength or with God's strength? The Lord offers us an all-inclusive insurance policy: Himself, unlimited counseling sessions, a *way* through life with all its potential problems, and unconditional love. And it's free . . . with infinite benefits. He's the only One that fully understands the obstacles, the problems we face. And, the only One with real answers. Reading *The Problem Solver* was like a cool drink. It helped me apply these truths to my own life."

Lynelle Hill
Registered Nurse
Deer Park, Washington

"There really is the ultimate Problem Solver, and I think that we should cultivate groups coming together to solve their problems using the inspirational and godly tools that we learn about in this book. The fifty-minute counseling sessions with the Lord changed my prayer life. And the yearly *Anno Domini* (wait until you read about that), will truly bless every year of your life — if you do it! And, you should do it! Enjoy meeting the amazing characters in this book, and wish you could be right there with them."

Lani Netter
Film Producer
Malibu, California

"I am bawlin' overwhelmed, chest filled with heartfelt joy and gratitude for having had the privilege of reading this book. One could feel that this is inspired text designed to teach, hone and fortify spiritual lessons. The book almost creates a new genre, where self-help meets allegory and can reach readers wherever they are in their personal walks with God. *The Problem Solver* is a well-paced page turner with identifiable characters who conjure up recognizable every-person emotions. This is a captivating novel that perhaps should have its own accompanying journal."

Marilyn Gill
Television Executive
Atlanta, Georgia

"*The Problem Solver* is one of the best books ever! It was like my own session with God. While I was reading, I began to connect the message of the book to my own life. I started deep thinking about my own problems and their solutions. When we have God as a Friend we can be calm. We can trust that the solutions He finds for us are the best. It's peace in our hearts."

Malgorzata Ravn
Artist
Odense, Denmark

"After reading *The Problem Solver* I feel refreshed. I feel as though I am friends with all the characters—including the wayward Gwen! It was a magical, inspiring, and spiritual story. It inspired me to look deeper into my own soul, reminding me that we are all here exactly where God wants us to be on our journey toward Him and Heaven. He will help us overcome all obstacles and give us His perpetual strength."

Carrie Moses
Grandmother
Portland

"*The Problem Solver* leads us from 'begging bowl' prayers into a relationship with God as our personal *Counselor*. My prayer time is now a scheduled counseling time: I can talk, I can cry, I can write, I can vent, I can merely sit in silent reflection. No expectations, no demands. He listens, and I feel His Care."

Christine Laws
Educator and Editor
Dahlonega, Georgia

"I had the pleasure of meeting Tom while hiking on the Camino de Santiago in Spain and I now consider him a good friend. He has captured the pilgrim's experience in *The Problem Solver* as it occurs in everyday life. I was amazed to hear that he wrote the book before actually making his pilgrimage. Few people have the opportunity to understand what life is like when guided by prayer. *The Problem Solver* shows how miracles just seem to happen all the time and if you are tuned in to seeing them, you notice. God brings you what you need. He puts the people in your path to help and guide you: the mediator, the advocate, the sage. If you are willing, he builds you a family. *The Problem Solver* reads like a modern-day gospel showing how truly close to God we all are. This book is full of moments of inspiration and consolation. Tom Gehring writes, "Your fountain shall overflow my friend, it shall. I promise. You are here for a reason." His allegorical story brings you inspirational lessons showing you that life through God has purpose. If you allow yourself to be his instrument you find joy and peace. I urge everyone to read this book. It helps us remember that coming to God can be such a difficult first step that seems so easy and right once it has been taken."

Carlos de la Camara
Schoolteacher
Camino de Santiago, Spain

"I've known Tom a long time. He's a lawyer and counselor. But his book, *The Problem Solver*, is about connecting with the real Counselor, the Isaiah 9:6 and Isaiah 28:29 Counselor, the Mighty God, and Prince of Peace. Read this book and be blessed."

Jed Nibbelink
General Contractor
Santa Clarita, California

"I am arrogant at times—probably more times than I care to admit. I did not think much of this book when I picked it up to read. But, this book showed me that I am Norm Adams, with a little bit of Harold Rosenberg. *The Problem Solver* inspired me to start having quiet time. It works and I would not have known the power and peace of quiet time with the Lord, but for this book. Read it."

Sharyn Alcaraz, Esq.
Corporate Legal Executive
Los Angeles, California

"*The Problem Solver* is an inspirational and a convicting book at the same time. It made me reflect back to when I was at that point in life when I had to make *the decision*: which line do I stand in, the one where I rely on God's strength, or the one where I rely on my own strength? I chose to rely on God's strength. As I read this book, I felt as if I was there in the story with each character, living each and every moment with them. The bottom line is that God will restore us and our relationships, and He will walk with us and never leave us. God truly brings people into your life to encourage you, pray with you, love you, cry with you, accept you for who you are and where you are in life, and never judge you. This is the type of God we get to serve. We all have thresholds in life, and you're at one right now. What are you going to do?"

Jason Layton
U.S. Marine
Encinitas, California

"I was amazed how these characters developed and how through their vulnerabilities my affection for them quickly grew. I could really identify with Norm as the parallels of his life and mine were so apparent. It felt like a personal victory for me when he chose to spend time with the Lord instead of going to the bar on his birthday. In addition, the concept of seeing my time with the Lord as a counseling session was amazing. That alone has revitalized my prayer life and brought back enthusiasm and focus to my time with God."

Doug Pellott
Fitness Expert
Sacramento, California

"I could so relate to each and every one of the characters in this book. We must remember that God is the ultimate Problem Solver and we should solve our problems on His strength. This is one of those books that you want to keep pulling out over and over again. When you read the same incident again, one keeps getting different 'life lessons.' Each of us needs to have 'counseling sessions' with the Counselor. God's plan for our life will always be better than our plan."

Joyce Springfield-Collins
Former Editorial Director, GRACE Magazine
Memphis, Tennessee

The Problem Solver

Everyone has a problem,
some reach for the solution

Tom Gehring

MONTSERRAT
PRESS

I know it is presumptuous to write a book like this.
But, I felt it best to just tell the story
as it happened and as I experienced it.
So many people were impacted by the Problem Solver.
And for reasons that became clear much later,
I was called to write this book.

In that regard, I have to thank Baby Doe 1, Nick Tate,
Harold Rosenberg, Tempie Teagarden, Bentley, Tikipas,
and of course,
the Problem Solver.

I tried to tell the story as clearly as I could.
I believe I got it right.

And, no matter what,
I believe.

Norm Adams

I WILL instruct thee
and teach thee in the way
which thou shalt go:
I will guide thee with mine eye.

Psalm 32:8 (KJV)

Note to readers: *The Problem Solver* is mostly taken from the notes, journals, and chronicles of the various people in the story. I held to the originals as closely as possible, so capitalizations (or lack thereof), use of pronouns, and various nuances are as in their original writings, and were usually intentional by the writer.

The Problem Solver

PART I

The Chronicle

1.

The Problem Solver

There once was a hurt and broken person
who had experienced a lot of pain and suffering in his life.
He was at his wit's end.
Indeed, he wanted to end it all.
What was the point of going on?
Why bother?
He was ready to give up. He was done.

But, he decided he would take one more
crack at solving his problems before ending it all.
What did he have to lose?

And so his new journey began.

The man actually did have a
lot of problems. His wife had just left him,
the kids were going with her,
he was having problems at work, and
his health was suffering. Just to mention
a few.

He had lost
interest in life, and he had no goals.

In reality he realized
that he had had problems his whole life.
Problems — were the only thing
he could rely on having
all the time.

The man decided to look
for the ultimate problem
solver.

One just had to exist. A counselor,
a psychiatrist,
a preacher,
a teacher,
a brilliant philosopher,
the ultimate friend.
Someone.

There must be someone he could look to
to solve his problems, or give him
a mechanism, a strategy
to solve his problems.
He'd pay for the answers.
Whatever the cost.

The young man started to ask around.
Did anyone know the perfect problem solver?
Could anyone suggest a good counselor,
a psychiatrist,
a preacher,
a teacher,
a brilliant philosopher,
maybe just a good old-fashioned friend.
Someone?

Perhaps he just needed a good doctor.
Someone who could give him
the right prescription.

Ironically, after asking all over town,
up and down the street,
wherever he went,
somebody did come up.
One of his work friends said
he should go see
the Problem Solver.
"Who's that?" the young man said.
"Well, he's this guy who set up shop
in the local courthouse. You can find him
in the upstairs
cafeteria.
He sits there on Mondays and
Fridays helping people solve their problems.

"They call him 'the Problem Solver.'
That's all I can tell you."

As the young man kept searching around town, the name "the Problem Solver" kept coming up. So, he decided that first thing Monday, he would go down to the old courthouse, take the elevator up to the cafeteria, and seek out the Problem Solver. What did he have to lose? Frankly, the old guy sounded a bit like a nutcase. Supposedly, he was this old guy who would spend Mondays and Fridays in the old courthouse listening to anyone who showed up, and he would solve their problems.

Over time, the judges would send some of their toughest cases to the Problem Solver to settle. And, he would settle them. Other times the judges would just send someone with a problem to the Problem Solver, and somehow, the problem would be solved.

It wasn't clear how, but, it was.

The young man couldn't wait until Monday. He was going to make sure he was at the courthouse.

He wanted to meet, *the Problem Solver.*

T+

2.

First Decision

It was Monday morning, 8:00 a.m., when the young man arrived at the courthouse. There was a line to get in, so he got in the back of the line and waited for the doors to open. He was anxious to meet this so-called Problem Solver. The young man certainly had his doubts that anyone could solve his problems. But he had made a commitment to try, one last time.

The courthouse doors opened, and the line started to move forward. *Thankfully*, thought the young man, *I want to get this over with*.

As the line got closer to the door, the young man could see everyone going through security, putting their briefcases on the conveyor belt, emptying their pockets, and going through the metal detector. Then the security guards saw the man in front of the young man.

"Hey, it's the Problem Solver, let him through." And everyone around the Problem Solver just made it quicker for him to go through.

All of the security guards exchanged pleasant greetings with the Problem Solver: "How you doing this fine Monday morning?" . . . "Great to see you Prob." . . . "You're looking good, as usual." . . . "Finally, 'TPS,' the man who gets the real work done, has arrived." And, in each case, the Problem Solver returned a nice hello and a smile.

And the young man watched it all.

The young man followed the Problem Solver to the elevator. The Problem Solver wore a weathered, but classic, gray herringbone sport coat, a white shirt, buttoned-down, weathered Levi's blue jeans, and wingtips, classic. All weathered, all worn, all earned.

The Problem Solver got in the elevator, and so did the young man. The elevator was full, but the young man was positioned next to the Problem Solver.

"Good morning, young man," the Problem Solver said.
The young man was startled. The Problem Solver was talking to him.
"Good morning," the young man said back. He spoke in a hushed tone, in the crowded elevator.
"Have you mde the decision yet?"
"What decision?" the young man said.
"Whether to solve your problems with God's strength, or your own?"
"What?" said the young man. "How do you know I have problems?"
"Well, that's why you're here isn't it?"

The young man was startled, again.

The elevator reached the ninth floor. The Problem Solver and the young man exited the elevator, with the few remaining passengers.

The young man followed the Problem Solver toward the cafeteria.

The Problem Solver looked over his shoulder. "So, have you made the decision?"

"What decision?" said the young man, hoping to avoid the question.

"Whether to solve your problems with God's strength, or your own?"

They continued walking to the cafeteria.

"No, I suppose I haven't," said the young man.

"Well, that's the first decision you have to make. And there's no in-between," said the Problem Solver with conviction.

The Problem Solver and the young man entered the cafeteria. The young man followed the Problem Solver to the middle area of the cafeteria. It was easy to see this was where the Problem Solver always set up shop. There was a long, simple cafeteria table with a few chairs around it. There were two lines already formed in front of the table, one on the left and one on the right.

The Problem Solver stopped walking, and looked at the young man.

"You must decide."

"Decide what?" said the young man.

The Problem Solver looked at the young man. He had sympathy. "I will say it once more, and then, that's it. . . . Are you going to solve your problems with God's strength, or your own? Now, think about your decision this week, and then, come back Friday morning."

"Friday morning? But I'm here now," said the young man.

"Don't you see the two lines?" said the Problem Solver.

The young man looked at the two lines that had formed in front of the table.

"Yes. I see the two lines."

"Well, I'm already booked for the day. You will need to come back Friday, after you've made your decision."

The young man was perplexed. He looked at the Problem Solver. "But I was here by 8:00 a.m.?"

"It wasn't early enough," said the Problem Solver. "There are people ahead of you in the lines."

The young man surveyed the situation. He looked at the Problem Solver.
"Why are there two lines?"

The Problem Solver was at his table by now. He looked at the young man.
"There are two lines because, one is for those who want to solve their problems on God's strength, and one for those who want to solve their problems on their own strength. I'll talk to anyone, but each one must make the decision. Including you.
"See you Friday."

And the Problem Solver sat down, and greeted his first person for the morning sessions.

And the young man stood there.

As he started to leave, he felt a stirring in his heart.

He decided he would be back Friday morning. Early.

And he will have made his decision.

T+

3.

The Right Place

It was Friday morning, 7:30 a.m., when the young man arrived at the courthouse. There was a line to get in, not much shorter than it was on Monday. But, he got in the back of the line and waited for the doors to open. He was anxious to finally get his first counseling session with the Problem Solver.

The courthouse doors opened at 8:00 a.m., and the line started to move forward. *Thankfully,* thought the young man, *I really need to get my problems solved as soon as possible. Preferably — eliminated, as soon as possible.*

As the line got closer to the door, the young man could see everyone going through security. This time he saw the diversity of the people: he noticed a young woman with a skier's cap on, unusual for a courthouse visit; he noticed nicely dressed professional men, obviously lawyers, one of them wore the same kind of business suit the young man prefers; he noticed a guy that looked like a burned-out old farmer, dirty, mud on his shoes, and close enough to smell, *badly*; there was a young guy, looks like an actor wannabe, long hair, tattoos; an elderly couple, man with badges sewed onto his shirt, wife with clipboard, holding hands until unbound by security so they were forced to go through the metal detector separately; he noticed anxious business people, with concerned and sober frozen faces anticipating a tough day in court; he noticed an amazingly common woman, head down, no life to her, *depressed*; and, he noticed some children being dragged into court like props by adversaries with a custody and support confrontation expected.

This truly is not a happy place, thought the young man.

As the young man went through the security line and then the metal detector, he looked around, and noticed the Problem Solver was still further back in the line. So, he decided he better make his way to the ninth floor and get in line before it's too late.

The young man got in a packed elevator. He noticed the young woman with the skier's cap on immediately pressed the button for the ninth floor. He noticed the determination in her face. Others, including the old farmer, pressed the numbers for a few different floors. A lady, pulling two kids with her, pushed the button for the second floor with determination similar to the young woman with the skier's cap. Her floor came quickly, and she and her two kids shot out of the elevator.

She looked prepared.

For something.

Silence prevailed for a moment as the elevator continued its ascent toward the ninth floor. There was a stop on the fifth floor, and the old farmer got out, taking the smell with him. *Thankfully*, thought the young man. There was another stop on the sixth floor, and the elderly couple exited the elevator, quiet, peaceful, but determined. Something involving that clipboard, and the badges, was about to spring into action. Norm tried to read the badges. No luck.

He smirked, *they look like they're going to save the world. Unlikely.*

The young man was now standing closer to the woman with the skier's cap.

She looked up at the young man.

"Are you going to see the Problem Solver?"

"Yes," said the young man.

She nodded and smiled.
He noticed a little pain there, in her smile.

The elevator reached the ninth floor. The young man, the woman with the skier's cap, and the other passengers exited the elevator. They all seemed to be heading in the same direction.

The woman with the skier's cap was walking next to the young man.
She looked slightly up at him.
"What line are you in?"
"I'm not sure yet. This is my first counseling session."
"Well, the left line is for those who are trying to solve their problems on their own, and the right line is for those who are trying to solve their problems with God's help."
"I see," said the young man.

They walked on further. The young man knew — he had to make the final, *final*, decision.

The young man looked at the woman with the skier's cap on. He noticed how she adjusted it as she got closer to the Problem Solver's table in the middle of the cafeteria. He noticed why she wore the cap, and he felt sympathy.

He wanted to ask her a question, as people moved faster toward the two lines already forming.

"What line are you in?" he asked the woman.

"The left line," she said.

And she got in line.

The young man stopped. He surveyed the situation. There was the table. What he hadn't noticed last time was the three people sitting on the side of the table where the Problem Solver would sit and face those that were in line. Whoever he spoke to, would be sitting in front of him across the table. He saw the Problem Solver's chair, and to the right of where he would be sitting, sat a man and a woman, and to his left, sat a woman.

They were waiting for the Problem Solver and greeting people as they got in line.

Maybe there's a difference between Monday and Friday, thought the young man, as to why he hadn't noticed the three people before.

He hesitated. And then he made his *final* decision.

He got in the right line, to the right of where the Problem Solver would be sitting and facing out. He looked over at the left line and noticed the young woman with the skier's cap.

She smiled back at him, and nodded understandingly.

And then the Problem Solver arrived and briefly greeted those in line. Then he walked behind his table and greeted the two people to his right, and the one person to his left.

And then he went to work.

The Problem Solver called his first person for the morning. He chose from the right line, which was the line to his left. When the choice was made, the two people seated to the right of him, and the person seated to the left of him got up and fanned out and started quietly meeting and talking to the people in line.

Those in the two lines were now invited to sit in chairs while in line, and the two people worked the left line, and the one person worked the right line. The young man looked over toward the left line and saw the woman with the skier's cap on, now sitting. One of the people approached her, and sat next to her and they started talking, confidentially. The young woman looked happy to see the person.

The person working the right line was sitting now with the person in front of the young man. He couldn't hear what they were saying, but they were talking comfortably and relaxed.

And then the person, a woman, got up and approached the young man.

"Hello, nice to meet you. I'm Intern One, I work with the Problem Solver on the right line. You are in the right line. Was that your intention?"

"Yes," said the young man.

"Good," said the woman. "How are you this morning?"

"I'm fine, just anxious to get on with quickly solving my problems."

Intern One looked at the young man. Her eyes connected with his.

"This is your first day. You still have to make it through your first day," she said, smiling, but with no commitment.

"What do you mean?" the young man asked.

"Well, you still have to talk to the Problem Solver," she said.

"Who are you?" asked the young man.

"Like I said, I'm Intern One, I work with the Problem Solver on the right line. Over there are Intern Two, and Intern Three, they work with those in the left line."

"Why are there two over there, and only one here?" asked the young man.

Intern One looked over at the left line.

"It's always harder to solve problems on your own strength. Problem solving takes longer over there."

"I see," reflected the young man.

"But, you made your first decision, you chose the right line. Congratulations. The second decision is coming up."

"The second decision?" said the young man.

"Yes, the second decision. I have to move on. There are no entries to go over with you, so I can move on to the next person in line. Just be patient, and your turn will come."

"What entries?" asked the young man.

"You haven't been assigned a Chronicle, so there are no entries to go over," she answered.

And just like that she stood up, and scooted her chair over to the next person in line. The person behind him was happy to see Intern One, and their discussion started out animated and happy.

And, the young man waited.

And watched.

And reflected on the First Decision he had made. A peace came over him.

He felt he was . . . in the right place.

This feels good. Something feels right.

T+

4.

Second Decision

Finally, it was the young man's turn. The Problem Solver called him over to the chair directly in front of him. The young man and the Problem Solver could easily look at each other across the standard-issue cafeteria table, positioned in the center of the courthouse cafeteria.

The young man looked at the Problem Solver, and said, "I have a problem."

"Indeed," said the Problem Solver. "You have many problems."

"How do you know that?" asked the young man.

"You've had no source for solutions," said the Problem Solver. "That's about to change."

The young man look baffled.

The Problem Solver looked into the eyes of the young man. "What's your problem, young man?"

The young man thought for a second and decided to lead off with what he thought was the most urgent one.

"My wife left me," the young man said with a certain righteous indignation.

"I see," said the Problem Solver. "And why did she do that?"

The young man leaned forward, with conviction, and said, "I don't know. She hasn't paid any attention to me for a long time, and she finally left."

The Problem Solver said peacefully, "Are you at least somewhat responsible for her leaving?"

"Me?" exclaimed the young man. "How could I be to blame? She left *me*. She had no reason to leave me. And take the kids! She took *my* kids. She's ignored me for years. Won't talk to me. Won't discuss what's the problem. Nothing!" And the young man sat back, realizing some people were close enough to hear if he raised his voice.

"Let me ask you this question, one more time. Just one more time. Are you at least somewhat responsible for her leaving? Yes or no?" asked the Problem Solver.

"Like I said, how could I be blamed for this?" the young man said in a loud, hushed tone. "I didn't do anything wrong. She just left. And — took the kids!"

"My question could be answered with a *yes*, or a *no*." And the Problem Solver looked at the young man with sympathy.

"Well, I can't answer the question with a *yes* or *no*! I thought you could help me solve my problems?" said the young man with consternation.

"Young man, this courthouse is filled with the lukewarms who can't answer simple questions with a *yes* or a *no*. They refuse to even hear the exact question. They spin all kinds of tales and mysteries, hoping for one advantage or another. Perhaps it's best if I just spew you out of here right now, because I can't get a simple *yes* or *no* answer."

"The question doesn't invite a *yes* or *no* answer," argued the young man.

"Young man, in short order, your wife will serve you with divorce papers, and you will have another reason to be in this courthouse. The second floor, in particular. That's when you will realize, *you've* lost your wife. *You* have — that's how it happened.

Now, I'm willing to help you with your problems, but you have to make a second decision."

"What's that?"

"You have to decide whether you are going to be ruthlessly honest with yourself. You got in the right line. You already decided to solve your problems with God's strength. Now, you have to decide whether you are going to be ruthlessly honest with yourself. — We're done for today."

The young man was dumbstruck. "That's it? Session over?"

"Yes," said the Problem Solver. "Over the weekend, decide whether you are going to be ruthlessly honest with yourself. If you can be ruthlessly honest with yourself, you can be honest with God, and with me. See you Monday."

The young man stood up. "What makes you think I'm going to come back on Monday?"

"There's only one source for answers. Do you think you'll find it between now and Monday?" said the Problem Solver.

The young man stood there.

The Problem Solver had another question for him. "Young man, do you still love your wife?"

"Of course I still love my wife. Even if she left me."

"Do you love your wife more than your neighbor?"

"What kind of question is that? Of course I love her more than my neighbor?"

"You shall not bear false witness against your neighbor. I suggest you don't do it against your wife."

The young man raised his voice: "I don't do it against my wife!" And he noticed others looking his way.

"Young man, when you begin to be ruthlessly honest with yourself, you can begin to make lasting progress for yourself, and with your wife. Would you like that?"

The young man was forced to think about it.

"Yes."

"Good, I would, too. And, there's no point in making the third decision unless you're committed to the second decision."

The young man paused. "Okay, the first decision was to decide to solve my problems with God's help and strength, and the second decision is to be ruthlessly honest with myself. Correct?"

"Yes," said the Problem Solver.

"What's the third decision?"

"Young man," said the Problem Solver, "don't rush things. Take your time over the weekend. Really think about this. Make the decision that for the rest of your life, *you are going to be ruthlessly honest with yourself.* And then, meet me back here on Monday."

The young man thought about it. He looked at the Problem Solver.

"Okay, see you Monday."

The Problem Solver stood up, looked the young man in the eye, and shook his hand.

"Young man, one last thing. Be vigilant this weekend. Any decision to change your life for the better and forever will come with resistance. Expect it. . . . But, it's a good sign."

And the Problem Solver called the next person.

And the young man started to walk away.

And — then he stopped.

T+

5.

The Group
Ruthless Honesty

The young man had just told the Problem Solver he would see him Monday. He said one thing, but didn't hear the other. He wasn't a good listener. He wouldn't be vigilant.

Frustration.

The young man stopped and stood there for a moment. Doubt set in.

He *thought*, random thoughts. He put value in random thoughts. Anger welled up inside of him. *I've been ruthlessly honest with myself,* he thought. *Who is he to tell me otherwise?*

It was early Friday morning. He looked around the cafeteria and decided to take a seat, and lick his wounds. *Nothing had been solved in his life. Nothing,* he thought proudly to himself. *This has been a waste of time.*

He sat down. He watched the Problem Solver talk to others who sat in front of him. There certainly were many people who wanted to see him. Both lines were long. And the three interns worked the lines as they moved forward.

He noticed the old farmer scurry into the cafeteria and quickly take a seat in the right line. The young man surveyed his clothes. *He probably stinks as usual*, thought the young man. *Perhaps I should offer to buy him a new shirt, a new pair of boots*, he thought smugly. *The guy looks penniless.*

He noticed the young woman with the skier's cap sitting close to him. She was writing in a notebook. The young man looked at her.

"What are you writing?" he smirked.

"I'm journaling. It took me some time before I was really ruthlessly honest with myself, but now that I am, I have a lot to say. I'm journaling." She looked at the young man. "Be patient, you'll get your notebook."

The young man looked around. He suddenly noticed that there were others close by who were writing in notebooks. He was staring now. Some of the people even had timers. What were they timing?

Strange, he thought.

"Honesty is just the most amazing thing. I had never really been honest with myself," the young woman said. "But now, it's different. And I'm writing it down, *everything*. I'm afraid these moments will pass if I don't write everything down . . . I don't want to go over this territory—ever again," and she sighed.

Just then the actor with long hair and tattoos walked up. He sat down. He looked at the young woman. "How's your journaling coming?"

"Fantastic," the young woman said. "I'm really making some breakthroughs."

The young man moved closer to the young woman and the actor.

Just then a professional man in a business suit looked over. "Hey, I got my notebook this morning."

The young woman and the actor smiled and laughed.

"Come on over," said the actor.

The professional man walked over and sat down.

The young woman with the skier's cap looked over at the young man.

"You know, you might as well come over. Meet a few of us in need of help."

The young man moved closer to the young woman with the skier's cap, the actor with long hair and tattoos, and the professional man in a business suit.

Just then a woman, in her everyday suit, walked up. "Excuse me, I was just told by the Problem Solver to join this group."

The actor with long hair and tattoos looked at her. "Of course, join us. Please! This is so exciting. I was hoping I would get into a group. I'm making so much progress! — But, I really wanted a group."

The woman, in her everyday suit, sat down.

And there they were:

The Young Woman with the skier's cap.
The Actor with long hair and tattoos.
The Professional Man, in a business suit.
The Everyday Woman, in her everyday suit.
And, the Young Man.

The Actor slapped his notebook down on the table.

The Young Woman slapped her notebook on top of his.

The Professional Man slapped his on top of the other notebooks.

The Everyday Woman, in her everyday suit, slapped her notebook on top of the other notebooks.

The Young Man looked at them. "I don't have a notebook yet."

The Actor spoke up quickly. "Slap your hand on top of the stack, and you're in."

The Young Man slapped his hand on the stack.

"You're in!" said the Actor.

They all smiled . . . and then laughed.

"I'm so happy to have found a group! Thank you all so much," said the Young Woman with the skier's cap.

There were "thanks" all around.

The Young Man looked around the cafeteria. He suddenly noticed that there were a lot of groups. He hadn't noticed this before.

He looked at his fellow group members.

"When do I get a notebook?" he asked.

The Young Woman with the skier's cap said: "When you decide to be ruthlessly honest with yourself."

The Actor looked at him. "It's simple man, you can't write one word, not one sentence in the notebook, unless you know in your heart you are being ruthlessly honest with yourself. Otherwise, this is all meaningless, and you will continue to be, as you are now, *frustrated.*"
The Young Woman smiled sympathetically at the Young Man. "Without pity, tell yourself the truth."
The Actor looked at the Young Man. "You're going to make it man."

Intern One was suddenly there. She put her hand on the Young Man's shoulder and surveyed the group.
She looked at the Young Man: "Congratulations, you made it to the ninth floor."

The Young Man looked at the group.

He smiled.

"See you Monday."

T+

6.

First Threshold . . . part 1

Monday morning. 8:30 a.m.

The Young Man stood outside the courthouse. He arrived at 8:00 a.m. He had watched the line go into the courthouse. Only the remnants of the line remained. New people got in line. He would have to cross the sidewalk, walk to the door of the courthouse, and go in . . . if he wanted to.

But he hesitated.

It had been a very long weekend. He had left the group meeting Friday morning so inspired. But, by the end of the day, he hesitated. It was hard being ruthlessly honest with himself. He thought of the Young Woman's words: *Without pity, tell yourself the truth.* He certainly had a lot of things to tell the truth about. His marriage, his job, his kids, his *issues*.

Work had been stressful, so by 5:00 he was ready for a drink and headed off to Chelsea's, his favorite bar. There was no reason to go home. His wife and kids had left him. They didn't even want to see him.

Within no time and a few drinks he was feeling much better. He ran into all his regular friends. They encouraged him. They heard he was free now. His wife and kids were gone.

Freedom.

And his job. "Forget about it," his friends told him. "Something better will come along. They don't deserve you."

The Young Man had forgotten what he had been so upset about. He was free now. He could do what he wanted to do.

Saturday was even better. He had to sleep in a little after the night before, but soon he was on the golf course with another group of friends. They expressed concern that his wife and kids had left him, but the Young Man assured them things were good. He was going to enjoy his newfound freedom.

By Saturday night he was having a hard time remembering what he needed to be ruthlessly honest about. So, no reason to stay home. He headed out to Chelsea's again.

And had a blast.

He left the bar at 2:00 a.m. Life was good again. He already had company. And she was pretty.

He was pulled over at 2:15 a.m.

T+

7.

First Threshold . . . part 2

Monday morning. 9:00 a.m.

The Young Man still stood outside the courthouse. There was no more line. New people showed up at the courthouse and just went straight in.

It had taken until late Sunday night to find a friend to bail him out of jail. He hurt to think of how many calls he made. He was finally forced to call a friend from work. He helped. He is the same friend who recommended the Problem Solver.

One thing was clear, his drinking buddies at Chelsea's — wouldn't help him.

His golf buddies — wouldn't help him.

By Monday morning, the Young Man knew, *they weren't his friends.*

And there it was, the first thing he admitted to himself. It had taken all weekend to tell himself the truth about just one thing. But he still couldn't avoid the self-pity.

Now my job is even more in jeopardy, thought the Young Man.

The shame welled up inside him. He had failed again. There was no point in standing there any longer.

He turned to leave.
He started to walk away.

"It's just a sidewalk."
The Young Man heard the voice in the midst of the Monday morning sounds, people shuffling along, cars passing, voices in the distance.

"It's just a sidewalk."
The Young Man heard it louder this time. He turned to look behind him.
And he saw the Problem Solver. And he felt joy. He didn't know the feeling. But tears started to flow.

The Young Man started to cry. "It's an awfully wide sidewalk." And he laughed through his tears.
And the Problem Solver shared the need to laugh. "It sure is sometimes, isn't it?"
"All the time for me," said the Young Man.
"All the time for some of us," said the Problem Solver.
"I often find that whenever I try to do something good for myself, it's like evil is right there with me . . . and that's the path I take. I was at war with myself all weekend long."
"There's no mystery to what I do," said the Problem Solver. "If there was it wouldn't be easily accessible to everyone . . . but it is. . . . Solving our problems is within all of our reach. I'm not going to suddenly disappear and reappear, and do magical things. You are real, problems are real. And, solutions are real, and solutions can be permanent. You just have a few more decisions to make."

They stood on the sidewalk for a moment. The Young Man looked at the Problem Solver. "You know, when I first came to see you I was hoping you would help me solve my problems quickly. Heck, I was hoping you could help me *eliminate them.*"
"The extent to which you want to eliminate your problems is usually the extent to which you don't want to take responsibility for them," said the Problem Solver. "You just want to eliminate them, not solve them."

"Which would help me avoid being ruthlessly honest with myself."

"Basically, yes," said the Problem Solver. "Why don't you come back up, I have a gift for you."

"Okay," said the Young Man. "You go ahead, I'll be up shortly. This is one threshold I have to cross by myself."

"I understand," said the Problem Solver. And he headed back to the courthouse, across the sidewalk.

. . .

One part of being ruthlessly honest with myself, thought the Young Man, *is to realize that solving my problems will take time. There is a big difference between solving a problem and eliminating it.* The Young Man thought further, *I suppose most efforts to 'eliminate' a problem are immoral, unethical, or illegal. You have to be very careful if you think you are 'eliminating' a problem. We're not talking about how to get a stain out of a sofa or finding the right floor cleaner.*

The Young Man was ready.

He crossed the sidewalk.

He would carry on with his mission to solve his problems.

It's just a sidewalk, he thought. *On the other hand, it's just one drink, it's just one bite, it's just one pill, it's just one flirt, it's just one lie, they're all thresholds. Don't fear the attacks, they're just thresholds to cross. They are opportunities – and I will take them from now on. Opportunities, to cross another threshold.*

He walked into the courthouse, went through security, hopped on the elevator, and pushed the button for the ninth floor. He was happy, and content.

Then the elevator opened. They applauded, they smiled, and they hugged the Young Man.

There they were:

The Young Woman with the skier's cap.

The Actor with long hair and tattoos.

The Professional Man, in a business suit.
The Everyday Woman, in her everyday suit.

And, the Young Man.

T+

8.

The Chronicle . . .
and, the Third Decision

Monday morning. 9:30 a.m.

The Young Man got in line. The right line. He sat down and waited his turn.

Intern One was suddenly there and she sat down next to him. "This is an exciting day for you, you get your Chronicle."

"My what?" said the Young Man.

"You get your Chronicle. . . . Be patient. Once you get your Chronicle, there will be times when I will go over your entries with you, and check up on your progress. It will be revealing and fun."

The Young Man looked at Intern One. "I have to admit, this is the strangest process I could have ever imagined. I simply don't know how to take this."

"It's okay. Your brook has run dry and you're *waiting* for water. Living water. You can either rush to find your own answers or, wait for your miracle. God's timing is perfect. I suggest you *wait*. Waiting is willingness. Your fountain shall overflow my friend, it shall. I promise. You are here for a reason."

"Intern One," said the Young Man intently, "who is the Problem Solver? Is he a facilitator, a mentor, a guide, a counselor, a friend, what?"

"I think he'd be okay with you calling him a counselor, with a small 'c.' There's another Counselor you will be getting to know better, real soon."

"Okay," said the Young Man.

"And, with that, it's your turn."

The Young Man saw the Problem Solver signaling him to come up. The Young Man stood up, walked over, and sat down in front of the Problem Solver.

. . .

"I have a gift for you."

The Problem Solver signaled to Intern One. She reached into her pouch and pulled out a notebook and handed it to the Problem Solver.

The Problem Solver looked it over. Smiled, nodded to Intern One, and she quietly went back to the line.

"Here it is," said the Problem Solver and handed the book to the Young Man.

The Young Man looked at the notebook, but, more than a notebook. The cover was in rich leather. The book was about nine by seven inches. And an inch thick. And on the cover it said:

1st Chronicle
The life and future of _____.

"This is where it begins *with* you," said the Problem Solver.

The Young Man continued to survey the Chronicle. It was beautiful. It already looked somewhat weathered, worn-in, old, been around. But, he knew it was his.

The Young Man looked at the Problem Solver.

"Where do I begin?"

"When you make the third decision. When you make that decision, write your name in the blank right there." He pointed to the blank line on the cover of the Chronicle.

The Young Man felt the weight of the Chronicle in his hands. It was actually quite light. *Meant to be taken anywhere*, he thought.

"After you make the third decision, and write your name on the cover, you write the decision on the first page of the Chronicle, and then the date, time, and place. Ask a few friends to witness your commitment. Ask them to sign their names there."

"What's the third decision?" asked the Young Man.

"Young Man, one of the reasons I came down to get you in front of the courthouse this morning was because I needed a walk. I had just spoken to the Old Farmer, and I was so sad . . . I needed to pray hard for him.

"The Old Farmer has been running a dairy farm in the central valley for close to five decades. He's well-known in that area. He's led many dairy organizations; he's been honored as Outstanding Dairy Producer of the Year, for many different years. Awards, trophies, and ribbons fill the walls of his little office in the central valley.

"But he's in danger of losing it all. The world's in a mess right now. Feed prices have increased by 50 percent this year alone, while milk prices have stayed low. He owes seven million dollars to his banks and creditors, and he's losing $35,000 every month he stays in business. He can't afford to feed his 1,000 cows and 800 heifers. Occasionally he's forced to sell some of his cows. Some of them are sold for slaughter.

"The Old Farmer doesn't like the city much. He's spent a lot of time in this courthouse and a courtroom on the fifth floor fending off a foreclosure lawsuit as he tries to hold onto his farm. And later today, he will meet with some bankruptcy lawyers. He doesn't see any alternatives.

"The man cried as I spoke with him this morning. He misses his wife. . . . She passed away last month.

"You know what is so amazing about the Old Farmer?"

"What's that?" said the Young Man as the story sank in.

"I don't know of one problem the Old Farmer has that is of his own making. And there's the big difference between you and him. *Your* problems are of your own making. You are the purveyor of your own problems. In many ways, you're in a much better position than the Old Farmer. And, yet, I rarely see a man with greater faith than him.

"Which leads me to the third decision you have to make today, tomorrow, or sometime before I see you again.

"You have to pray for the Old Farmer.

"The third decision is you have to decide to be a person of prayer. And your first assignment is to pray for the Old Farmer."

"But, I don't even know the Old Farmer," said the Young Man.

"If you knew him well enough to think harsh thoughts about him, you know him well enough to pray for him," said the Problem Solver.

The Problem Solver continued, "To offer to buy him a shirt, or a new pair of boots? . . . You might as well stick a dagger in his heart.

"The *sidewalk* he has to cross will require a miracle."

"I understand," said the Young Man.

"I can't tell you how the Old Farmer has blessed me," said the Problem Solver. "He told me this morning, despite all he has gone through, that he will *wait*. He sees waiting as an action verb. His *waiting* is alive with faith. I'm blessed to know him, and you will be, too," said the Problem Solver.

The Problem Solver gestured to the Chronicle in the Young Man's hand.

"It will take some time to learn how to use the Chronicle. You go forward backward with your entries, and backward forward with the names of those you are praying for. And eventually you will meet somewhere in the middle of your Chronicle. Remember this, your Chronicle is *not* a journal, it is not a diary. It is your Chronicle. It is to be transparent. If anyone were to pick it up, you would be proud of what is written there. You have much to be thankful for. And it is here in your Chronicle you will have much to record. Including the miracles that will come your way. Just like Jehoshaphat, you will *recall the ways* that God has helped you.

"I know God has plans for you, plans to prosper you and not to harm you. Plans to give you hope and a future. Those plans are worth recording. Those plans can be seen by the world.

"I'll see you Saturday."

And with that, the Problem Solver signaled for the next person.

As the Young Man stood up, he looked at the Problem Solver and asked him: "How do I pray?"

"How to pray? That's why you have your group. They are waiting for you," said the Problem Solver.

"Thank you," said the Young Man, and he turned to walk away. Then he stopped and spun around.

Saturday? What did he mean by 'Saturday'? But the Young Man saw that the Problem Solver was already talking to the next person. *I'll be back on Friday, not Saturday,* thought the Young Man.

But it was time to look for his group.

T+

9.

The Group
Prayer

The Young Man looked for his group. He passed a table and noticed the Old Farmer was sitting with a group of four other people. *Five people, like my group*, he thought. He surveyed the group, *and just as diverse as my group*.

He saw his group and headed toward their table. The Actor was the first to jump up and greet the Young Man.

"Hey everyone, look who's got his first Chronicle!"

There were greetings all around as the group congratulated the Young Man.

"Here's how it works," said the Actor. "To get started, you decide if you're going to be a person of prayer. You're going to do it man, praying is easy, it's just talking to God. And don't worry, you're not telling him anything he don't know, he knows everything. But, praying is an act of humility! It gets the process going. You're going to love it, I promise."

The Young Woman leaned forward, "And, don't forget, when you make the decision to be a person of prayer, write the commitment on the first page of your Chronicle, and we get to sign our names as witnesses. It's powerful. We're there for you."

"I see we all have a notebook, but only the Actor and I have Chronicles," said the Young Man.

"They're left liners. They have journals, we have Chronicles," said the Actor.

The Young Woman sighed. "I'm simply not ready for God. Not even sure he exists. He wasn't there for me over and over again when I needed him. And now, since I'm so sick, what's the point? It's over for me soon. I'm done anyway." She lifted up her journal. "I've journaled every hurt, pain, loneliness, trial and tribulation I've ever gone through. It's helping. That's all I can say. It's helping."

The Everyday Woman, in her everyday suit, patted her shoulder. She looked at the Young Woman. "I have to be honest with you. I'm thinking of asking the Problem Solver if I can switch over. Every day I have to fight off, fend off, or struggle with depression. It is sometimes every minute, sometimes every breath, but every day I have to fight depression. *Every day* — is just another day trudging through the valley. I've never had one day — that I thought of as a 'gift.' I originally chose the left line. And, this journal has really helped. But, I think I'm ready to ask the Problem Solver if I can change lines. I can't do it anymore. I need something more than my strength. *I* . . . just don't have any strength left."

They looked at the Professional Man.

The Professional Man, in a business suit, sat forward. "I'm sorry I haven't participated much. . . . My problem is, *mediocrity*. I'm in my forties and . . . I've done *nothing* — in a world that thinks I've done everything. I'm successful. So what? I can't even find a purpose. How can I do that, when I have everything? What's the purpose of searching for a purpose if you don't need a purpose? I have a great profession, but all I really did was fall into place where everyone expected me to, wanted me to, or demanded me to. Either way, here I am. I can't imagine any greater transition than saying 'no.' No more. If I keep going down this path, what you see now, is what you will see in thirty years, only older. Much older. Much more unhappy. I'm just one short step away from starting an addiction, an affair, a disaster. This is where I see many of my rich and famous clients ending up. . . . If I were the devil, I would just shower people with success, money, and prestige. I would bring down half the people. Or more."

The Professional Man leaned back in his chair.

"I'm lukewarm about anything and everything.

"Here's the discussion with my wife on Saturday: 'What do you want to do?' 'I don't know, what do you want to do?' 'I asked you first.'"

He looked at the group. . . . "Don't worry, I don't expect anyone to feel sorry for me. Do you even want me in your group? I don't even want me."

"Yes, they want you," said the Problem Solver who was suddenly there. He sat down. "They want you to stay."

Everyone confirmed.

"We need each other," said the Actor.

"And I need you," said the Problem Solver.

They all looked at him with surprise.

"Yes, I do," said the Problem Solver. "I need all of you next Saturday. Here's my request:

"You all meet me next Saturday at the Outreach Center, 9:00 a.m. I will need you all day. You will meet a lot of great people, and there will be plenty to celebrate. So, instead of coming Friday, please come Saturday."

The Problem Solver looked at the Young Man first. "Young Man, instead of coming here Friday, I want you to go to work at 7:00 a.m. on Friday. 7:00 a.m. sharp. And when you get there. You pray over your desk, and your surroundings and your fellow workers' desks. And you think of three things that will improve your employer's business and decide that you will implement those three items. . . . You're going to be president of that company one day . . . okay?"

"Okay," said the Young Man.

"And one last thing. Before Saturday, you are to have one counseling session with the Counselor. *The* Counselor. I've asked the Actor to explain how it works. Okay?"

The Young Man looked confused, but he said:

"Okay."

"You will know when it's time for the counseling session. You will get the feeling. That's the Holy Spirit talking to you. When it happens: *listen*. And start your first counseling session. Trust the Holy Spirit."

"Who?" said the Young Man.

"It's okay. For now, just trust your heart," said the Problem Solver.

The Problem Solver looked at the Everyday Woman. "It's time. I want one hundred for Saturday. You know what I mean. It's time. This will save you. Bake them up. And inside of each one of the cups, just like we discussed, put a message. You can do it. Your peace muffins are the best muffins I've ever tasted. I need one hundred of them, with a message slipped into each cup . . . agreed?"

The Everyday Woman looked a little scared. "Agreed."

The Problem Solver looked at the Actor. "Your job is to help the Everyday Woman, with special emphasis on the messages. I need one hundred muffins, with one hundred messages, one in each muffin cup. You will help with the messages. She'll show you how."

The Actor clapped his hands. "Easy, no sweat. I'm in."

The Problem Solver looked at the Professional Man. "You are to bring *it* Saturday. You are going to play all day Saturday. All day long. This is serious. There's a lot of people who are hurting. *Hurting ears are not critical.* You will bless them."

The Professional Man was concerned. "But, I've lost my chops. I don't think I have it in me anymore."

The Problem Solver nodded. "You do. Your adventure starts — Saturday. Bring it . . . and play. Play your heart out — *play your heart out.*"

There was a deep sigh, from the Professional Man.

"Okay," he said.

The Problem Solver looked at the Young Woman. "I'd like you to consider getting your home in order and packing a small suitcase. I think you may want to spend a few nights at the Outreach Center. The accommodations are comfortable and you will be surrounded by loving and good people. Will you consider it?"

"Yes," said the Young Woman.

"Good," said the Problem Solver.

The Problem Solver looked at the whole group.

"Thank you. I will see you all Saturday instead of Friday. Intern One will give you directions. Please exchange telephone numbers and addresses. You may need to be in touch with each other. Saturday's a big day. Bless you all."

And with that the Problem Solver stood up and walked away.

The group took a deep breath together and began to exchange telephone numbers and addresses. Then they started to say goodbye.

The Young Man stopped them.

"I'll need some witnesses here.

"I've decided to be a person of prayer, so I need some witnesses."

"Okay," said the Young Woman, as they all gathered around.

The Young Man wrote his name on the front of his Chronicle. And then went to the first page, and wrote down his commitment, dated it, and signed his name.

And one by one, his friends, his witnesses, signed their names and set forth the date.

The Young Man looked at the names.

There they were.

The real, the worldly names, of:

The Young Woman with the skier's cap.

The Actor with long hair and tattoos.

The Professional Man, in a business suit.
The Everyday Woman, in her everyday suit.

And, the Young Man.

There was cause for hugs.

"One last thing," said the Actor. He looked at the Young Man. "Stay a little longer, I'll give you some thoughts on your first counseling session with *the* Counselor."

The Actor and the Young Man said goodbye to the other three.

And they all agreed. They would see each other next Saturday.

The Young Woman, the Professional Man, and the Everyday Woman left.

The Actor and the Young Man stayed a little longer.
And talked.

T+

10.

The First Prayer

The Young Man was home.
It was late Wednesday night when the telephone rang.

The Young Man answered the telephone. He recognized the voice. It was the Everyday Woman.
"Yes, it's me," she said as she cried. "I'm having a tough time tonight. I just can't do this anymore. . . . Will you help me?"
"How can I help?" said the Young Man.
"Will you pray for me?" said the Everyday Woman.
"Okay, but, to be honest, I've never prayed for anyone," said the Young Man.
"Well, I've never asked anyone to pray for me. But this is it for me. I can't go on."
"Okay . . . I'll pray for you," said the Young Man.
. . .

The Everyday Woman waited.
"You mean, now?" said the Young Man.
Through tears, the Everyday Woman said, "yes."
. . . "Okay, here goes.
"Dear God, I don't know where to start, but I need to talk to you. I'd like to pray for my friend. Lord, she has depression. And this depression Lord, is killing her. Lord, I know what it's like to have something that's killing you and you just can't control it.

My drinking, Lord. You know what I'm talking about. Anyway, I'm here to pray for my friend, Lord. Please take this depression out of her life. We speak to her depression and say 'Be gone! In Jesus' name. Gone, forever, in Jesus' name. Never to return.'

"Father God, I speak out for my friend. Lord bless her, bless her life. And Lord, tell her to do it, just make the decision. *Move*, do it immediately, move to the right line. She's going to make the decision to turn her problems over to you, Lord. She's going to move to the right line. Lord, but this depression, I'm coming against it now, in the name of Jesus. It's gone *now*, Lord. In the name of Jesus, gone, and cast into the sea *forever*.

"Now, Lord, it's late, let her sleep. Lord, please give her rest and peaceful dreams.

"And I ask for all of this, in Jesus' name.

"Amen."

. . .

"Thank you," said the Everyday Woman.

"You're welcome."

. . . "Not bad for the first time," she said.

"Thank you," said the Young Man. . . . "Have you spoken with the Actor? He was going to help you."

"No," she said. "He's tried to call. I didn't take his phone calls. I was in a slump, and couldn't get out."

"Well, you will make it 'til the morning. And at 9:00 a.m., the Actor will knock on your door. Be ready for him. You have a lot of baking to do. You'll get it done."

"Okay," said the Everyday Woman. . . . "I know where you'll be in the morning."

"Where?" said the Young Man.

"At your office at 7:00 a.m.," she said. "You were supposed to start Friday, in two days. But you've already started, haven't you?"

"Yes," said the Young Man. "It's time for me to go the extra mile. I'm determined to come up with three things every morning that will improve where I work. That's a lot of changes by the end of the day Friday."

"Well, you be there at 7:00 a.m. And I'll make it until 9:00 a.m. Deal?"

"Deal."

"I knew in my heart I could call you. Thank you," she said.

"Goodnight," said the Young Man.

"Goodnight," said the Everyday Woman.

The Young Man hung up. And then picked up the telephone again.

And called the Actor.

T+

PART II

The Surrender

11.

Second Threshold . . . part 1

Friday night. 6:00 p.m.

The Young Man was home. He sat at his kitchen table. He looked down at his Chronicle. He looked at his name "Norm Adams," written on the cover, filling up the blank space.

1st Chronicle
The life and future of Norm Adams.

What's the point? he thought. He's thinking he should stay home and have his first counseling session, with *the* Counselor. But why? He feels called to do it, but he would really prefer some confirmation. Maybe what he's feeling is wrong. *Just a feeling.* Not that important.

Go ahead, ignore it.

He has a second threshold to cross. After four days of going in early, he was on top of his job. He can do this . . . he feels *self*-empowered. He doesn't need to surrender. It's his birthday, another year — gone. It's time for him to get a break. He doesn't even need to go tomorrow. There's no need.

He's back. He's sure that woman is there from his last visit to Chelsea's. She's always there.

She's waiting.

He can't go out tonight and hope to be at the Outreach Center first thing in the morning, especially with a clear head.

But, it's his birthday, and where are his wife and kids? Why aren't they here?

He saw some mail that might have been a card. Hmmm— *That's it?*

He looks down at his Chronicle again. It feels a little strange to see his name there. He had written it. There it was. His name. This was, or is, the Chronicle of his future. It is to be transparent. He recalled the words of the Problem Solver: "If anyone were to pick it up, you would be proud of what is written there. You have much to be thankful for. And it is here in your Chronicle you will have much to record. Including the miracles that will come your way."

The only entry so far in his journal was a commitment to prayer, witnessed by four friends. He looked at the first page of his Chronicle. There was his commitment. There was his signature. The signature was dated. There were his witnesses. His four new friends.

But . . . so what?

Norm sat at his kitchen table. He stared at the ceiling.

What is a *birthday?* He thought about how old he was.

When he called the Actor Wednesday night, the Actor agreed to be at the Everyday Woman's home the next morning, 9:00 a.m. He was looking forward to it! He already had lots of the messages written in his heart that he would put in the muffin cups.

Then the Actor reminded the Young Man how to have his first counseling session with *the* Counselor, the Lord. But tonight, the Young Man hesitated. The Problem Solver had told the Young Man to have one session with *the* Counselor before Saturday morning.   But, he hesitated.

He knew what to do . . . but, he wouldn't do it.

What's the point? he thought.

The Young Man had a great week. Things were good. He decided — he's going to treat himself.

He's feeling good. He freshens up. Looks in the mirror. He's looking good. He even looks refreshed. He hasn't felt this good in a long time.

He heads toward his front door.

He opens the door, he turns out the light.

As he closes the door, the telephone rings.
He shuts the door a little harder than usual.
That felt good, he thought.

He's outside.
But he hears the telephone ring anyway. Again and again.

T+

12.

The Second Prayer

Friday night. 6:30 p.m.

The Young Man headed toward his car. He was determined. But he could hear the telephone ringing from his home. No problem—he wasn't going back in. He was heading out. He decided, he was going to treat himself.

It's his birthday.

He got to his car. Then he was reminded, his staff had given him a car wash for his birthday, for all the extra work he had done all week. He stood in the driveway for a moment to admire his car. He was looking good; even his car was looking good. He thought of that woman; she's there for sure.

She's always there.

Then his cellphone started ringing as he opened the door to his car. Perhaps it's his buddies at Chelsea's. This was the call he wanted. He's sure his buddies hadn't forgotten him. Why had he been so hasty to assume they weren't his friends? They were just busy. That's why they couldn't help him last week. He understands.

He answers his cell phone.

"Norm here!" said the Young Man.

. . .

"Norm here!!" he said again.

"Norm, it's Tempie. Tempie Teagarden."

Norm heard the voice of the Everyday Woman. He was disappointed. Did he really give *all* his phone numbers to the group?

"Tempie?"

"Yes, it's Tempie. I hear the disappointment in your voice. Are you okay?"

"Yes, I'm great, things are going good. Couldn't be better."

"You're outside, where you going?"

"Oh, I'm just going to hang with friends. My buddies want to see me."

"Well, okay, but don't forget about tomorrow. 9:00 a.m. We're all meeting at the Outreach Center."

"I haven't forgotten about tomorrow, but really I don't — "

"Norm, don't say anything. I called you for two reasons."

Norm stood next to his car; trying to decide whether to hang up.

"Norm, it was so cool, Nick Tate — you know, the Actor — showed up yesterday, Thursday morning, just like you promised. He's amazing. Get this. We baked Two Hundred muffins! Two Hundred!! The Problem Solver wanted one hundred, but we baked Two Hundred. Two Hundred! Do you hear me, it was so exciting."

"Yeah, I hear you," said Norm Adams. He started pacing; he always starts pacing when he's losing patience. He admired his car. Shiny, with racing stripes. A lady catcher, all the way.

"Anyway, I need to tell you two things. Okay? . . . Hello?" said Tempie Teagarden.

"Yeah, yeah, I'm here," said Norm. He was on the sidewalk now. He looked back at his car. With the door still open.

Tempie knew: *Keep talking.*

"Norm, so anyway, Nick Tate and I start baking, and Nick starts praying as the muffins are coming out of the oven. And then the messages start flowing. On each message he makes a statement and then puts a verse under it. Get this, he brought the coolest little message paper, with beautiful borders, some green, some purple, just about two inches square. He writes the statement on the top, and then the little verse below. Then he folds it in thirds, and we slip them into the side of the cup each muffin is in. It pokes out of the cup — so you can see it easily. We have a decorated bag for each muffin. This was all Nick. And I did the muffins. — Norm, please tell me you're listening."

"I'm here." Norm is now pacing back and forth on the sidewalk. Another sidewalk. Another threshold. He looks back at the open door to his car. He could see the two tones of the rich leather under the interior light, the paneling, the high-tech dash.
. . .

"Norm, so it gets better. I started praying with Nick: *Lord, please place on our heart the exact statement, the exact declaration on each message, and then, the verse from Your Word, right under each declaration. Lord, please, let this all be from You. Please, Lord!*

"And, you know what?"

"No, what?" said Norm.

"We just kept baking. We didn't stop until we hit Two Hundred. I have never, ever, never, ever, been so — *not* depressed. And, by the time we were done, at the end of the day, we had Two Hundred muffins, with two hundred messages, and each of them in their own little bag, two hundred small bags.
. . .

"But! I'm not done."

"Look, my friends are waiting, I have to go." Norm was pacing faster now. The sidewalk seemed to be smirking at him.

"Norm! Please, I'm almost done," said Tempie. "So anyway, get this: about 3:00 p.m., my mailman stops by. He smells all the baking, so I offer him a muffin. And he's so excited he wants to try it right away. *'Like now,'* he says to us. And Nick and I get so excited. So, he opens the bag and smells the muffin, and takes it out of the bag. — Yes! And then he notices the message sticking out of the muffin cup just a little. And he says: 'What's this?' And I say, 'It's a message, a declaration just for you.' Norm, I was so nervous as I watched him slowly open the message. The border of the message was purple, so I know *I* had written it, with Nick's help. Anyway, this was . . . well anyway, he slowly opens the message. And he reads it. . . . And he slowly crumbles to the floor, and starts crying and crying. *And, crying.*

"Norm, are you there?"

"Yes, yes, I'm here, I'm listening." Norm Adams was now standing next to his car. But, as soon as this story is over, he's gone. His buddies are waiting for him. Off to Chelsea's.

"It took Nick and me minutes to console him. And by now, I'm devastated. What did we do? We've crushed the poor man. I've destroyed the mailman. But the mailman wouldn't let us have the message. Which one was causing him so much grief?

"Then he composed himself, and the first thing he said to Nick and me was 'Thank You.'

"And then he started to stand up, still clinging to the message. And then—he started crying again and said he was going to hold on to this until his son returned. 'Until my son returns,' he said. He said his son is a drug addict living on the streets and he hadn't seen him in a year. —He's seventeen years old, Norm. His son is seventeen years old! . . . I had written that message, and Nick helped me with the verse:

Your son is in My hands.
Don't worry, I will protect him.
"I know my sheep, and my sheep know me—"

"Norm, he was crying as he left. He said he was going to hold onto this message 'until my son returns.' *Oh mercy, Norm.* Now what? Norm, I wrote that message. I felt it so strong in my heart when I wrote it. And then Nick, gave me the verse. Oh mercy. I'm so glad Nick was there. I was panicked, joyous, sad, happy, excited, scared, all at once. Oh mercy. But Nick told me the message was for him, for *the mailman.* God wanted it—for him. So I calmed down.

"So, Norm, that's the first thing I had to tell you. Now, please let me tell you the second thing.

"Norm?"

"Yes, yes, I'm here. But really, I should be leaving soon." He felt a breeze blow a little dust through the air. Norm shut his car door. He didn't want the interior lights to wear down the battery. Or, get dust in his newly cleaned and detailed car.

"Norm, just one more minute, then you can go.
"Anyway, just as strongly, just a little while ago, I felt I had to call you. I have a request."
"What's that?" said Norm. Another breeze stirred up. Just a little stronger. Good thing he had shut his car door.

"Let me pray for you," said Tempie Teagarden.
"No, no, really, I'm okay, I don't need any prayers right now."
"But Norm, you prayed for me Wednesday night. It brought me out of the pit. Norm, I had never, ever, never, ever asked someone to pray for me—but, you did. You did. Now, please. Let me pray for you. I have never, ever, never, ever asked someone if I could pray for them. But, I'm asking you now. After all I saw yesterday. Please, let me pray for you."

"Well, okay, but I have to be heading out."
Norm opened his car door again. He was ready to leave. Tempie hung on.
. . .

"Now? You want to pray for me *now*?" said Norm.

"Right now," said Tempie.

Norm sighed deeply.
"Okay."

Tempie started in.
"Lord, thank You so much for yesterday. Please bless the message for my postman, and everything that comes about because of it. And Lord God, thank You, thank You, thank You, because I have never, ever, never, ever had a day like this, *with no depression*. None whatsoever. *None*. Nada.
"Anyway God, this is it. The first time I have ever asked someone if I could pray for them. So please put the words in my heart, and You, through me, just let it flow.

"Lord God, I pray for my new friend Norm Adams. Father God, let him hear You in his heart, like I did yesterday from You. Tell him exactly what You want him to do tonight. Tell him where to go, and what to do. Tell him who to be with, and who not to be with. Lord, tell him that his two children will return to him, and that his wife is waiting to see the joyful and incredible change in his life. *Repent* means to *change*.

"Lord, I pray that Norm knows in his heart all the plans You have for him, plans to prosper him and give him a future. Let him know that he will be an incredible blessing to so many people he will never be able to count them.

"Lord, please bless my friend Norm Adams. I pray for sweet blessings for him tonight and a deep and restful sleep so that when he sees us tomorrow, he's just booming with enthusiasm and strength that he has never felt before. Let this night be a night of healing, transformation, and peace for him.

"I pray all of this for my friend, Norm Adams. And Lord, I will see him in the morning and I will give him a big hug for this gift. A gift You gave me, Lord.

"The gift of letting me pray for him. What an amazing privilege! This gift of being able to pray for someone.

"Amen," said Tempie, as she finished.

. . .

"Amen," said Norm. As he stood next to his car.
"Amen," said Tempie, again.

And she hung up.
And Norm Adams, held his phone in his hand.

. . . And hung up.

And a swift breeze hit him in the face. Then, it was no longer a breeze, it was the wind.

A violent wind.

T+

13.

Second Threshold . . . part 2
and, the Fourth Decision

Friday night. 7:00 p.m.

When Norm hung up his cellphone he started walking. Perhaps he would just walk to Chelsea's if he had to. Then he realized he was standing in the street.

He just stood there. He looked across the sidewalk and saw his car. The car door was still open.

And the wind kicked up. It hit him hard, again.

Could he fight this wind?

He had to cross the sidewalk to get to his car. Here he was again.

Now he had to decide whether to cross the sidewalk, shut his car door, and go back into his house. Or, get in the car and drive away . . .

He was aware of only one thing. He had always chosen to drive away. This time, just possibly, it was worth not driving away. Just possibly.

He walked to the edge of the sidewalk.

And he crossed it.

And then he shut his car door . . .

Somewhere, down deep in his heart he heard, *never forget this moment, I shall remind you.*

A few minutes later, Norm Adams sat at his kitchen table again. It was time. Yes, he did feel it in his heart. Whatever that feeling is. He had to admit, he knew it. It was time.

He looked down at his Chronicle. He looked at his name again written on the cover, filling up the blank space. The space wasn't blank anymore.

So he decided to make the fourth decision. He hadn't even put the words in his heart yet. But he knew he had to make the fourth decision.

To surrender.

And to have his first counseling session with the Lord. He opened his Chronicle. He saw the first page where he had made his commitment to prayer and he saw where his friends had signed off as witnesses.

So, he chose the second page of his Chronicle to have his first counseling session.

This is what he wrote:

June 1, Friday
Norm Adams

Counseling session 1, with the Lord.

Okay Lord I made it. Here I am. I have to admit, this seems a little absurd to me. I'm having a counseling session with You — I guess somewhere in my heart. I set my timer. For fifty minutes. Why? What's this all about? I'm supposed to just listen for *Your* voice. Well, here I am. Where are You?

I'm here, at my Chronicle. Writing in my Chronicle. On page two. I don't have much to say. All I feel is hurt inside. My chest, Lord, is hurting. I feel like I could have a heart attack at any moment. I guess it's just stress from work, even though this week I've come so far, I know what I haven't done. I've seen all the things I haven't done. All the people I've hurt, some don't even know how I hurt them. They don't even know of my disregard. I see it all. The veil has been peeled back. My heart is so heavy. Lord, give me some time before I drop dead of a heart attack. Give me time to make things up to people. Give me just a little hope. I promise I'll be better. Why should I go on? I still feel that feeling hitting me hard. Bam, right in my gut. Get distracted fast, so I don't have to feel that feeling. Go out, my favorite bar. My buddies, a new girlfriend. I won't have to think about anything. I won't have to face anything.

Well, I'm here. And I have thirty-six minutes left in this session. Yes, I'm timing it. Because, I want to leave. Head out. Be with my friends. Meet that girl. Be with that girl. Have a few drinks. A few more. I can get rid of this hurt on my own. I don't need to be lonely. People like me at Chelsea's.

Thirty-four minutes and fifty-nine seconds left in this session, my first session and then — I'm gone. I need to be gone. This hurts.

"Norm."

. . .

"Norm Adams."

Yes?

"I'm really here. And I want to talk to you. Would that be okay?"

Yes.

"First, stop looking at the clock. Just spend a little time with Me. Just right here, at your kitchen table. Just stay awhile and be quiet. I'm not here to tell you what to do, or where to go, I'm here now to ask you to just stay awhile with Me. And be still. Will you do that?"

Yes. But I can't help looking at the clock. I'm sorry. It's easier to think this will all be over soon, and I can just do *my* own way.

"If that's what you want, it's okay. But consider just staying here with Me and just write down your thoughts, and My thoughts for you. Will you consider doing that?"

Yes.

This is kind of a weird feeling, Lord. Just sitting here with You. I mean, I think I can hear You in my heart. That's weird. I never stopped like this. Just to listen. This is so hard. Everything about me wants to run, scream, do something. Distractions are clamoring for my attention. I feel like Tempie must feel at times. Depressed, like I can't have a clear mind. A mind free to just . . . listen to You.

"Norm Adams. Do you know I give you the very air you breathe? The very next breath you will take. I number the hairs on your head, and I number the days you will have here on earth. Consider just spending a little time here with Me tonight."

Okay. I'm sorry. I'm here. I'm present.

I say it again.

I'm present.

Lord, I've never heard this sound. What is it?

. . .

"Just listen. Don't define."

. . .

Lord, can I stay here awhile? What is that? What is that washing over me? That's new.

. . .

Can I just stay here awhile?

Lord, I feel like a lot of things are being washed out of my life. What is that? It's okay. I don't really want to know just yet. It feels good to let things go. All I know, is I want to stay here awhile. And be with You.

This is strange. I thought You'd give me this big list of all my mistakes, all my stupid choices, the bad things I've done. What a gift. Why would You even want to spend time with me?

I actually set a timer. Now, I'm worried it will go off, and my time with You will be up. I have a new worry! Yes, that's what I'm used to. Finding something to worry about. To fret about. To obsess over.

"Relationship is easy. Especially with Me. I promise. This is the easiest thing you can do."

What is that I hear? What is that?

. . .

I've just never heard that . . . what is that?

This stillness. This peace. I don't know how to handle this Lord.

I don't want this to end. Lord, I hear You. I hear You so clearly in my heart. I can't believe it. But, it's so obvious to me. Here You are. I guess I have to accept that . . . You really do love me. Me. Norm Adams. Who am I? I'm a nobody. Why even bother with me?

Lord, . . . I want to serve You.

Somehow. I don't know what You could ever want from me? What do I have to offer? Nothing. Not a thing. Nothing. But I do know this. I'd really like to serve You. Be with You more. Something feels so washed out of me. What is that? What was that?

Lord, whatever that is, or was washed away, I don't want it back. Please don't ever let it come back.

. . .

What is that sound?

What is that stillness? That quiet.

. . .

My mind seems clear. What is that? I'm drying my eyes with the tablecloth. It seems joyous to me. I'm laughing and crying at once. What happened to me? This doesn't feel like Norm.

What is this renewal? What is this?

. . .

"Norm Adams."

Yes, Lord. I hear You so deeply in my heart. This part, right here, right now, how can I put this part in words? Simple little English words. I can't do it. I know I can't. I'm not going to try.

Oh . . . the timer just went off. Fifty minutes just went by.

But I don't want the session to end.

Can I sit awhile longer?

Lord, I just have one request.

Can I serve You?

Lord, I can hear so deeply in my heart what the fourth decision is. Amazing how obvious it is. No one has to tell me. You are telling me. Oh, Lord, I'm so sure now. You have so much for me . . . I feel it so deeply. I'm so thankful.

I cross this threshold. I make this decision. I write down this decision: Lord, I surrender all to You.

Thank You, Lord. Thank You.

. . .

Amen. Amen. Amen. I say to You. Amen.

Lord, thank You for this session. Thank You for this gift. Thank You.

End of counseling session 1, with the Lord.

T+

14.

Surrender

Saturday morning. 6:00 a.m.

Norm Adams woke up. And he laid there in his bed. *It was gone*, was his first thought. What happened to it? The tightness in his chest that had been there as long as he could remember. He looked at his Chronicle on his nightstand. This would never be something to hide away somewhere. Here it would be. Close at hand. Public for anyone who wanted to look through it.

1st Chronicle
The life and future of Norm Adams.

So many thoughts poured through his mind. He had so much to hide. He lived a life that couldn't be exposed in any way whatsoever. What's the opposite of that? Why would he want so much, so many things, in his life, that he had to hide, keep out of sight, not to be seen? Could he even live one day where his very thoughts could be seen by the world and he would be okay with that? Maybe even proud of that. Maybe even see the healing in that. How does one take his thoughts captive—to something better, something pure, something . . . peaceful?

He wanted to know.

He picked up his Chronicle. He walked to the kitchen table.

And sat down.

He read his entry from last night. He realized that this was his first full day of . . . *surrender*. What does that mean? He opened his Chronicle. And wrote.

This is what he wrote:

June 2, Saturday
Norm Adams
Surrender, Day One

Good morning, Lord.

That's all that comes to mind, right now . . .

Can I talk to You, just like this? Hmmm. What is this? Peace, I suppose. Can I really do this? Turn my life over to You? To You?

I think of the words, "I", "me," "myself." What exactly have "I" done that I should be proud of? Yes, I can think of some good things. But, if the world knew all my little secrets, then I end up with what I have now. Nothing. I think of my beautiful wife. My two kids. Where are they? And whose fault is that? I have so many best friends: drinking comes to mind first. *What a great friend he's been. I can really count on him.*

I would give anything to let that friend go.

This Chronicle is supposed to be forward-looking. Transparent. I guess I better stop writing now. There's just too much trash to throw out. So much trash. It would take the first half of this Chronicle. I'm sorry Lord, for . . . so much. Do you want a list? Just pour it all out right here? Is that what You want?

I know what's on my heart, right now.

It felt so good to have a counseling session with You last night. I have to admit, that was so weird. What was that?

I just listen. Well, I think I actually heard You in my heart. Wow! Is that true?

Is that You?

Lord, can I have another counseling session with You? Is there a limit on how many?

Counseling session 2, with the Lord.

Fifty minutes. I set my timer.

Here I am, again. Who knew I'd be doing this. Strange. I'm sitting at the same kitchen table I've sat at so many times. But this is different. I never noticed the tablecloth my wife made. It's beautiful. Deep blue. I never noticed the words she embroidered: "Over the table of the Presence they are to spread a blue cloth." What does that mean?

I never noticed what I could see through the kitchen window. The trees. The birds. The window faces east, and I can see that the sun is coming up, and blazing through beautiful clouds. This is cool. What a great window. I looked through that window so many times.

But . . . I never saw anything . . .

Where was I?

This day feels different than yesterday.

. . .

Everything feels different. Lord, here I am again. But already I feel like "I'm" getting in the way. Distractions. Thoughts. *What else should I be doing?* This feels out of place.

"Norm, I am here. I promise."

Lord, is that really You I hear in my heart? I'm sorry to question You. It's just that I, so don't trust my thoughts. I don't trust whatever ripples up through my thinking process.

How, oh how, can I discern, the good from the bad? The *You*, from the not *You*.

"Norm, stop thinking. Don't lean on your own understanding. Just be here awhile with Me and be at peace."

Okay, I can do that.

I'm sorry, I just looked at the timer: Thirty-seven minutes, forty-five seconds. Hmmm. Do I really want this counseling session to be over? There I go thinking again.

Lord, I have so many questions. How do I do things on Your strength, not mine? How do I surrender?

. . .

I hear You so deeply in my heart, I know the answer . . .
But I can't put this in words.

"Norm, this isn't work, this isn't lists, this isn't analysis."

There's that feeling again. And, what's that sound? What
is that quiet? I've never heard that.

What is this peace — I can't understand this.

. . .

This is truly a new day. I want so badly to look at the timer.
This is hard in some ways. I suppose I'm afraid of some things
that might come trickling up. But You said, *no lists.*

You mean I don't have to list all my mistakes, all my
failures, all the hurts I spread around?

"No. I'll take those on for you."

Really? That makes no sense to me. That, well, it just makes
no sense to me.

"Norm, this Chronicle is a great gift for you. It's My gift.
Soon, you will be writing, declaring, and living your future. All
that I hope for you. And all that you could ever be."

So, keep going, no matter what?

"Keep going. I'm always with you."

Okay. I can do that.

. . .

The first thing I see about my life from this day forward is:
Less, less, less.

There's so much I can cut out. Things I don't need. Things
that have gotten in the way. I know: no lists.

Lord, can I just talk about one thing? I can't help it.

It's . . . well. I'm thinking of my cool car sitting in the
driveway. It's only six months old. Brand new. It's beautiful. *It's
all I ever wanted.*

I love the color. Wow! It just jumps at you. And the racing
stripes. It's definitely a *lady catcher*. Every motivation to buy that
car was wrong. I know, *no lists*. But I think of the things I put off,
and needs I didn't meet for my family when I bought that car.
Wow, it's so pretty.

Why, this morning, not even twenty-four hours later does
it seem so meaningless?

That leather is so pretty. It just stands out. It makes a statement. Such a statement.

Some statements say nothing at all.

There's no substance. All *statement*, no substance.

. . .

Okay, I shall go on.

Well, Lord, I am human. I need input. If so much is gone, or will be gone. Where to now? What do I replace it all with? Lord, can I have a new kind of list? Maybe *Your* list.

. . .

"Yes, you can have a list."

Thank You.

"Here's your list for the day."

Okay.

"GTDL:

"One. Norm, let your light shine through. I want to see the biggest smile possible on your face all day long. Is that okay?"

Yes, Lord. I'll do it.

"Two. You already know in your heart what you are going to do today. I just ask you to surrender, to *whatever* I put in your path today. Number your days, Norm."

I will, Lord.

"Third. Call Baby Doe 1, right now. You know her as Zoe Singer. She needs you."

Zoe Singer? *The Young Woman*. One of the members of our group?

Right now? But our session isn't over.

. . .

Oh!! My timer just went off. *Interesting*.

Okay, okay, I'll call her.

End of counseling session 2, with the Lord.

Norm Adams looked for his list of numbers and found the number for the Young Woman in his group. He called the number immediately.

Zoe Singer's telephone began to ring.

Norm was anxious.

"Hello?"

Norm Adams heard the voice of the Young Woman.

"Zoe, this is Norm Adams."

"Norm?! . . ."

Zoe began to cry. "Norm, I collapsed last night. I'm so sick. Oh, Norm. All I've waited for was today. I even packed. I need to be with you all at the Outreach Center. But . . . hospice is here, and a doctor. They won't let me go. Norm, what difference does it make? . . . Norm . . . I don't have much time."

"Zoe? Is there anyone else with you? Family, friends?"

"No, just hospice and a doctor. They're very nice, but they won't let me leave. They won't release me without family." Zoe whispered: "But I don't have family."

"Zoe, why? What happened? What . . . what went . . ."

"Norm, It doesn't matter.

"I need a future that doesn't live in the past.

"Norm, I don't have any family.

. . .

"Norm, will you be my brother today?"

T+

15.

The Outreach Center . . . part 1

Saturday morning. 9:00 a.m.

Norm Adams heard something beautiful as soon as he emerged from his car.

He listened. *Stunning*. Music engulfed the area around the Outreach Center. In the distance, he saw people dancing. *But's it's 9:00 a.m.*, he thought.

Then with great care, he lifted Zoe Singer, from his car, and placed her gingerly in her wheelchair, and adjusted her ski cap.

Bentley, Zoe's hospice caretaker, was upset. He stooped down to speak to her.

"Zoe, you shouldn't be here. You should be in bed, resting."

"Bentley, soon . . . I will have plenty of time to rest."

Bentley shook his head.

Norm was excited: "Let's go!" And with that he took the handles of Zoe's wheelchair and started pushing her toward the wide-open entrance of the Outreach Center.

Zoe looked up into the air: "Where's the beautiful music coming from?"

"I don't know," said Norm. The sidewalk started to look busy with people as Norm, Zoe, and Bentley gushed toward the wide open entrance to the Outreach Center. They went through

the arch, with the sign above: "Outreach Center," and the small sparrow logo. So little so certain.
And there was Pastor Jonathan, directing people traffic. As best he could.

And then they saw their friends, Tempie Teagarden, Nick Tate, and the Problem Solver.
There were hugs all around and concerns about Zoe.
The Problem Solver looked at them: "We have a lot to do today. First, let's go see the other member of your group."

There's a certain type of electric harp that a young boy of twelve asked his parents for. The electric harp was designed by an Austrian, Hans Grundershun, and the symphonic sounds the harp produces can't be duplicated by other craftsmen or inventors — despite their best efforts. Highly chosen and crafted wood, strings, metal, and electronics from different parts of the world can't be put together by science, only by art and the hands of one artist.
Grundershun wanted a sound that couldn't be duplicated. Not by other brands. Not even by the same brand, different harp.
He achieved that.
The one who plays it is the one who molds it.
One harp, one artist.
One note, one brushstroke.
Never share a canvas, never share your harp.
Guard your heart, guard your harp.

The Professional Man's parents flew him to Austria when he was twelve, and purchased a Grundershun Electric Harp, No. 00101 for him as a birthday present. And he played it every day, whether at home, in bands, small orchestras, and solo, until he graduated from law school at age twenty-five.
After that, he hardly played. Eventually he put it down.
Until today,
. . . at the Outreach Center.

The night before, at the same time that Norm Adams sat down at his kitchen table, the Professional Man, Harold

Rosenberg, sat at his desk in his home study.

He looked up at the soaring shelves filled with books, photographs, awards, certificates, trophies, humidors, and intentionally open decorative spaces waiting for the next certificate of accomplishment, and thought about whether he would go tomorrow to the Outreach Center.

He decided no, he wouldn't. *Why bother? Is there any point in reaching back in time?* he thought.

. . .

Then he agonized over his elusive pain. He thought about his spouse down the hall in the master bedroom. Something he had always wanted, wasn't working. Longings buried deep are still there. The other rooms were empty.

. . . And, he heard something in his head he hadn't heard in a long time. Tears came. He remembered the music, and the joy it brought.

What was going through his mind?

He decided to do what the Problem Solver suggested.

He wrote.

This is what he wrote:

June 1, Friday
Harold Rosenberg
Guard your heart, guard your harp

Counseling session 1, with the Lord.

Okay, I'll put the timer on. Fifty minutes. A fifty-minute session.

Just for the record, I don't believe in God. *You*, if you're listening.

I don't have a Chronicle. I just have this journal.

This seems a little strange. I'm supposed to have a counseling session with the Lord, even if I don't believe in "the Lord," "God." Whatever.

I hear in my head things and sounds I haven't heard in a long time. I fear reopening that door. I put it away a long time ago. It's done.

What is that? Why has all this been laid on my heart. Why does it nag at me? Why?

This is stupid. That's all I want to say. This is a waste of time.

. . .

Still sitting.

Good, 42:33 minutes left. I'm passing the time anyway.

. . .

I don't know why I went to see the Problem Solver. I guess it was easy. I'm in that courthouse all the time anyway. So, no big deal, just go up to the ninth floor. Easy.

35:40 minutes left. Good, I'm burning up the minutes. . . .

At least I'm writing with my favorite pen. I love these Montegrappas. Crafted in Italy. I have them in beautiful colors. And I make sure I have the very special MonteVerde ink cartridges for them. The pen writes itself, I just do the thinking. Or do I?

I met Sergio Montegrappa once. In Italy. I went to his shop. He took his Montegrappa, and customized it just for me. The finest touches make all the difference. This pen has been through a lot of trials with me, court trials and otherwise.

Thank you, old friend. I remember back when Sergio originally customized this. I remember his words:

"Mr. Rosenberg, there shall be a special gold band in the middle and each one of your pens will be sequentially numbered. I'm starting with No. 00101." This is my favorite pen. I'm holding the first one. More were to come. But this is the first.

Purple.

I guess this is okay. Just chatting with "the Lord." If he exists. Do you exist? Well, what's the downside? I always ask that as a lawyer. *What's the downside?* I can't really see any downside in trying to have this little talk with . . . *the Lord.*

I'm looking at the band and there's the number. No. 00101. Sad, have I ever really looked at this pen? I'm just noticing something else.

Pr 1:33.

No — all these years. I never really looked at the pen.

I remember Sergio saying to me, "Use this pen to write, but use your heart to listen. What use is it to write, if you don't listen?"

Sergio told me: *"Listen to . . . God. Live in safety and be at ease."*

Proverbs 1:33.

I've lived in safety. In *pathetic* safety. Just look at my bookshelves. There is just too much risk in the type of "safety" I've carved out for myself.

But, I've never been at ease.

Never.

And, I've never listened to God.

Never.

Sergio made thirty-one pens for me. And each one has a verse from Proverbs. I had forgotten. But I always come back to this pen. The first one. Here it is.

. . .

I don't know how to listen. What should I be listening for?

And it comes flooding back. My fourth pen. No. 00104. Here it is.

Pr 4:23. I remember now: *Guard your heart, for it is the wellspring of life.*

I know what I'm thinking, but I don't want to deal with it. It's my life. I can leave it behind if I want. What's the big deal?

This is stupid, this whole counseling session idea. What is this? Write, write, write. Who cares. This journal would make good kindling. And my thoughts would be erased forever.

. . .

"Harold, I'll make you a deal."

Okay, I wrote that down, because I heard some thought pierce through my heart. *I may . . . still have one.*

"Here's the deal: Go downstairs to the basement. Pull the cover off your harp. Hook it up. And turn it on. And I will speak to you. But not, with words. That's the deal."

Okay, I wrote that down. Those are words I understand. I guess a little discussion is okay.

20:55 minutes left.

I know what you're thinking Lord. I hear you. *The number's the same. My first pen and the harp.*

I suppose it wouldn't hurt to go downstairs and turn it on. Why not?

Okay, I'll go. . . .

. . .

Okay, I'm back upstairs.

The timer is at 00: 10. Just ten seconds left.

. . .

Okay, I admit.

You win.

"Harold, remember:

"Even dreams have valleys.

"Go tomorrow.

I will be with you."

. . .

End of counseling session 1, with the Lord.

Saturday morning. The Outreach Center. 9:15 a.m.

The music was getting louder, people were swaying, even dancing.

And there they were:

The Problem Solver.

The Young Man, Norm Adams.

The Young Woman, Zoe Singer, with her skier's cap, in a wheelchair.

The Actor, Nick Tate, with long hair and tattoos.

The Everyday Woman, Tempie Teagarden, in her everyday suit.

And, the hospice caretaker, Bentley, ever watchful of Zoe.

They made their way toward the music.

And they saw their friend, the Professional Man, sitting at an electric harp, playing, eyes closed, and his whole body, arms and fingers, engaged and at one

. . . with the harp.

No. 00101.

The harp was plugged in and staff at the Outreach Center had brought out amplifiers and speakers. Others had joined in, there were conga players, marimbas, a stand-up bass player, a guitarist, drums, a flute, and other instruments. And, people swaying and dancing. The Outreach Center was alive with the music. Several vocalists joined in. Impressionism. Improvisation. And they all followed the Professional Man. They knew the key.

The audience grew as the group joined the smiles of many people.

"How can a man named 'Harold' play the harp like that?" said a man standing behind Norm Adams.

Norm looked back at him: "That's my friend, that's Harold Rosenberg!"

"I never heard songs like this," said the man.

Even the Problem Solver had a tear. "Recognition of the heart . . . and the other musicians see it."

And the music played on.

Norm Adams, felt something so deep in his heart. He missed his wife. His kids. *What is this?*

He suddenly saw all that was going on around him at the Outreach Center. The center of the Outreach Center was just bustling with activity: He saw craftsmen fixing, hammering, building things, and he saw the elderly couple, man with badges sewed onto his shirt, wife with clipboard, observing, taking notes; he saw doctors giving medical attention to children; he saw dentists looking in people's mouths; he saw ladies at sewing machines mending clothes; he saw barbers and hair-dressers cutting hair; he saw peaceful lines of people lined up for all the free services offered by so many smiling people who had a trade — to give away, to bless people, to touch people, to heal people, to feed people;

to . . . and then

. . .

Then Norm heard his friend Harold's harp take a beautiful turn. He recognized the first bars of a song he had heard his whole life and he knew the history of the song. And Harold knew the history of the song as he played it. And he knew it should be played here, at the Outreach Center. And how so many years later after its release in 1967, it would bless so many to sing it. Tim Hardin, who wrote and recorded "If I Were a Carpenter," died of a heroin overdose on December 29, 1980, at age thirty-nine.

Norm shook his head. Harold knew what he was doing. Give a nod out to someone else who struggled.

All the other musicians joined in . . . one by one they knew the song, and they bonded in rhythm, key, notes, and lyrics.

. . .

Then a man stepped up to a microphone and began to sing some lines, as Harold and the other musicians played on

'If I were a carpenter
and you were a lady
Would you marry me anyway?
Would you have my baby?'

. . .

And Norm saw a craftsman at his booth. He could see that his trade was fixing musical instruments. And then he saw young boys and girls, and others of various ages, and saw that they came to get their guitars fixed, new strings for a cello, a flute needed some glue, drum sticks had been customized for a young musician with a goal in mind. And the sparrow logo would be placed on the instrument. So little so certain. And Norm saw a young woman smiling as the craftsman handed her a violin, fresh strings, and the bow, reset,

And the girl put it to her chin

And in perfect synchronization, played her violin, eyes closed, tuning in

She joined the song being played

Long strokes of the bow across the strings . . .

'If a tinker were my trade,
would you still find me
carrying the pots I made — following behind me?'

And Norm watched a young boy rush in with his bongos and join as the song played on, and more and more voices joined the lyrics:

'Save my love through loneliness
Save my love through sorrow
I've given you my only-ness
Give me your tomorrow.'

And Norm heard everyone singing now

'If I work my hands in wood,
Would you still love me?
Answer quick, Babe: *yes I would* — I'd put you above me.'

And Norm saw Harold finally open his eyes. There was joy in both men's eyes.

'If I were a miller
At a mill wheel grinding
Would you miss your color box?
Your soft shoes shining.'

And the notes of the girl's violin soared off the walls of the Outreach Center.

'If I were a carpenter
and you were a lady
Would you marry me anyway?
Would you have my baby?

'Would you marry me anyway?
Would you have my baby?'

Music lifted, voices lifted, and the song came to an end with all being part of it. Everyone clapped, there were hugs everywhere. Harold Rosenberg stood up. All the musicians hugged him, much before the group could get to him.

But they did.

And there they were:

The Young Woman with the skier's cap, in her wheelchair.
The Actor with long hair and tattoos.
The Professional Man, in a business suit.
The Everyday Woman, in her everyday suit.
And . . . the Young Man.

Words weren't necessary.
Just hugs.

T+

16.

The Outreach Center . . . part 2

Saturday morning. 10:00 a.m.

There was just one line.
The right line.
Norm Adams looked at the Problem Solver, "Why is there only one line?"
"Down here, everyone figures it's best to solve their problems with God's strength. They already tried everything else. Down here is when up there didn't work.
"Your job today is to counsel with the people in the line as they work their way up to talking to me. You are Intern Two today."
Norm looked confused. "I'm an Intern? I don't know anything about counseling. I'm not qualified."
"Counseling is less about qualification, more about inspiration.
"Let me introduce you to Intern One."

And with that, the Old Farmer presented himself. He looked at Norm Adams. He smiled a big ol' smile and grabbed Norm at the waist and lifted him up with his strong arms and hands.
"So nice to meet you. I'm excited to work with you today, Intern Two. It's an honor." He held out his hand as he delivered Norm back to the ground. "My name is Tikipas."

"Norm Adams. Nice to meet you," Norm said, looking up at Tikipas.

The Problem Solver said to both of them: "Okay, it's a long line today. Each of you take a side and alternate counseling with those in line as they work their way up to talking to me.

"Serve until you're healed, and then keep serving to stay healed."

And with that, the Problem Solver went to his table at the front of the line, the only line, and told the first person to come forward and sit in the chair in front of him.

Tikipas nodded at Norm Adams. "Let's go, Intern Two."

Norm felt shaky. He took a pause. He surveyed the Outreach Center.

He quickly found his grounding:

He looked over to the center of the Outreach Center square and saw that Harold Rosenberg was sitting again playing his harp with the other musicians, the music was soft but resonating, supplying the support for all that was going on around them;

A short distance away he saw the Everyday Woman, Tempie Teagarden, and the Actor, Nick Tate, passing out peace muffins, the line in front of their table was long, but he saw in a flash that two people at a time were taking and sharing one muffin between them, and the message became a mutual blessing and prayer and so, where two or more are gathered, they knew something special would take place;

And further off, he saw the Young Woman, Zoe Singer, in her wheelchair, with Bentley next to her. She was in a circle with other women, some also in wheelchairs. Women of all ages and color, women of the same hope and dreams. Hands and arms were animated; discussions were transparent.

And Norm smiled. Across from him, on the other side of the line, with another person was Tikipas, animated, smiling, talking, and . . . listening. No word would miss his heart or gaze. His dirty clothes and shoes were a banner and he was a witness.

Okay, Norm thought, *here I go*. Norm sat next to a person in line. The person looked at Norm, really looked at him.

"My name's Stephen. So—you're the one I'm supposed to talk to," said the first person for Norm to counsel with.

"Me?" said Norm as he surveyed the young man, about seventeen years old.

"Yes, this is exciting!" said Stephen. "I hit it last night, I'm really excited. My One Hundredth counseling session with the Lord. Do you know how significant that is?"

"No, I don't," said Norm.

"It's so cool, I've been here six months, staying here at the Outreach Center, and I hit my One Hundredth counseling session with the Lord, last night. It was fantastic. Anyway, get this, he told me just as I was ending my session to tell the Intern in line that he, God, would restore your marriage and family. Just like that. That's it, that's all I got. But it was clear, man."

"Are you married?"

"Yes," said Norm.

"Whew! That makes me feel better—you have to step out in faith whenever that happens, you get a *word*. I had only done two sessions with the Lord, when I felt he told me to make it—to one hundred. Man! I wanted outta this place," said Stephen as he lifted his gaze to the Outreach Center. "I wanted out, but I felt the Lord said 'make it to one hundred, as long as it takes—and, I did it last night. It took six months."

"You've been here six months?" asked Norm, wondering how, oh how, he could possibly counsel Stephen.

"Yes. Off the streets six months. Living here. Off heroin, off crime, off being me. It feels good.—How many counseling sessions with the Lord have you done, man it must be a ton?!" Stephen said.

"Two," said Norm.

"Fantastic! Man, you're at a transition point. This is it. You're good to go. Make it to One Hundred. A hundred means *full*, it signifies return, the principle of return. 'And other seed fell upon the good earth and having sprung up it brought forth fruit a hundredfold. . . .'"

Stephen was standing now, shouting. "Thank You, Lord, for healing me!! THANK YOU, LORD!!"

And everyone around applauded Stephen as he sat back down.

"What's your name, man?"

"Norm."

Stephen leaned forward. "Norm, here's the thing. Make it to One Hundred, set a goal. I promise you, your marriage and family will be restored. God's already gone before you. This is exciting! And for me, I can't wait to see what the Lord has in store for me. I know the very next thing I have to do. Go back to my father, apologize, and ask for forgiveness. I think I have the courage now."

"You do," said Norm. "Indeed, I think your father is here today."

"Here?! Today? Impossible, he's a postman. He has a route on Saturday."

"I know, but I think he's here today."

Stephen paused. "Why?"

"I think it has something to do with a muffin," said Norm.

And Stephen saw that it was his turn.

And they stood up and hugged.

Stephen looked at Norm. "You're an amazing counselor."

And the Problem Solver called Stephen forward.

. . .

Saturday afternoon. 2:00 p.m.

By the daring afternoon of the high reaches of the Outreach Center a subtle breeze began to blow through. There was a pause for the longest moment, and everyone looked up.

. . .

"It's best to be reminded every once in a while . . . to be ready," said the Problem Solver.

Most people seemed to hear him from where he was standing behind his table.

And then, slowly, everyone went back to what they were doing. And Norm looked at the last person in line for him to talk to. He refocused and looked at the man.

The man adjusted his chair and sat up. He slowly unfolded some notes he had. He looked at Norm and began to read. This is what he read:

"Hello, my name is Chase.

"I've had an abusive relationship with words my whole life.

"I've used words to abuse my family, friends, strangers, just about anybody, and mostly myself.

"In my first counseling session with the Lord, He asked me to take a vow of silence for one week. I was not to speak for one week unless I first wrote down the words, and thought them through. I was to first determine if my words would speak life into someone . . . or me, before I could even read my words to the person.

"I've now gone forty days. And, I have been blessed to *truly know* that death and life are in the power of the tongue. And . . . I choose *life*.

"And then, this morning, when I was praying, I felt the Lord told me to break my silence with the Intern in line this morning.

"That person is you.

"This is what the Lord told me to say."

Chase folded up his notes, and carefully put them away. He looked at Norm.

And began to speak.

T+

17.

The Outreach Center . . . part 3

Saturday afternoon. 2:30 p.m.

Chase slowly got ready.
To speak.
He hadn't done it for one month. Not uttered one word. Commitment had to be finalized before he said the first word. This was start day for him. This day would be a new day. All the days going forward would never again be like the days before.

And it all had to do with the words chosen. His heart had been quieted over the past month.

The Lord had asked him to go one week. Chase went for more than one month. He had never known such peace. What was this?

He felt the movement of his mouth. The muscles that would be employed if he said even just one word. He really didn't want to. To break the silence.

Norm sat there. He saw Chase struggling. He saw.
Chase looked up. Couldn't he go just one more month? Could he get permission?
No.
He was to speak. He looked down. He made a commitment. For a lifetime. He wrote something in the dirt. Then looked up and spoke:

"In the beginning . . .

"was the Word, and the Word was with God,

"and the Word was God. He was with God in the beginning.

"Today, right now, this moment, is my beginning, my new beginning. I'm so blessed to know the power of the Word. Each word we choose. Words were used first to create, then to communicate. I will press on now. To reach the prize, to reach the victory. I am so thankful."

Chase looked at Norm.

"The Lord came that you may have life, and have it more abundantly. The Lord intends to bless you, pressed down, overflowing, more than you can imagine. In one year, you will enter into a time of life.

"Life more abundant.

"He who does not love, does not know God.

"Norm, I am blessed to know you. My prayer for you is to have life, and to have it more abundantly. And, I'm adding you to my prayer list. I'm close to the middle of my Chronicle.

"Peace, my brother."

Chase and Norm stood up. And hugged.

Tempie Teagarden was there. Standing next to them.

She looked at Chase and Norm.

"Here it is, my last peace muffin.

. . .

"I'm so blessed . . . I baked Two Hundred, it still wasn't enough. And then, as everyone shared a muffin, one became two, and sometimes two became four. And the message was shared."

Tempie looked at Norm. "Norm, I saved one for you and your friend."

She handed the small bag with the muffin inside to Norm.

Norm looked at Chase. "We shall share this."

Norm opened the bag. Took out the muffin. Handed the muffin message to Chase, and then split the muffin in half.

Chase read the message.

Norm read the message.
They looked at each. Then nodded.
This was a message that would come again . . . in due time.
In stories planned, but still to be written.

Don't let your story go unwritten.

And they ate.
. . .

The Actor came rushing up. Panicked. He tried to contain himself.
He was crying. Then crying hard. Really hard.
"Our friend. Zoe. Has collapsed. She's not breathing. They're trying everything to revive her!
"We called an ambulance.
"It's on the way."

T+

18.

The Hospital

Wednesday night. 6:00 p.m.

Norm Adams burst through the hospital door and bounded down the various hallways heading toward Zoe Singer's hospital room. Zoe had been in the hospital since Saturday afternoon. The group had carried on the vigil since then, taking turns, sometimes together, sometimes alone, but always to make sure someone was with Zoe, if she woke up. If she rallied.

Norm had gotten in to work every morning at 3:00 a.m. so he could get to the hospital when and if necessary. His reputation at work had soared.

But, an hour ago, he received a call from Tempie. Zoe was barely breathing. She was expected to die any moment.

Norm arrived outside Zoe's hospital room. Everyone was there:

The Actor, Nick Tate,
The Professional Man, Harold Rosenberg,
The Everyday Woman, Tempie Teagarden,
and now, the Young Man, Norm Adams.

And then the Problem Solver arrived, Tikipas, and others from the Outreach Center. There were chairs outside Zoe's room, so Norm sat down to catch his breath.

Tikipas suggested they get in a circle and pray. And they did.

Norm listened to the prayer and thought about the people he was with. He barely knew them. But he knew them. And he knew Zoe. And he prayed hard with the others.

Bentley came out of Zoe's room with the doctor. Norm could tell they didn't have much to say.

Bentley was crying. He asked them to keep praying.

And they did.

Wednesday night. 8:00 p.m.

The doctor came out of Zoe's room.

"She's still breathing," he said. He had tears in his eyes. "What's keeping her going?"

Wednesday night. 10:00 p.m.

The group was still there. No one was going anywhere.

The doctor and Bentley came out of Zoe's room.

"She just took a couple of breaths. They were a little stronger.

"I'm . . . I don't know what else to tell you."

"Pray," said Bentley.

The doctor looked at the group. "I'm still assuming she doesn't have any family, is that correct?"

"We are her family," said the Problem Solver.

"We are her family," everyone said at once.

The doctor looked at Norm Adams. "Bentley said you're her brother."

"I'm her brother," said Norm Adams.

"I'm her brother," said Nick Tate.

"I'm her brother," said Harold Rosenberg.

"I'm her sister," said Tempie Teagarden.

Tikipas stood up. "And I'm her friend," said Tikipas.

The doctor looked at them.

"I see," he said. "Well, some decisions will have to be made soon."

"May I see her?" asked the Problem Solver.

The doctor looked at Bentley. Bentley nodded.

"Okay. But keep it brief."

And the Problem Solver went into Zoe's room. He carried a small wrapped package with him, and had his pouch slung around his shoulder. Only Norm noticed.

Wednesday night. 10:15 p.m.

The Problem Solver sat next to Zoe. Zoe was barely breathing. Yet, there was a peace about her. He spoke to her.

And one knows when one can listen.

"I'm sorry I'm just getting around to giving you this gift." TPS looks at Zoe and places the wrapped package, complete with a bow, on her bed stand. "Don't worry, there's *one more* where that came from. You'll understand later.

". . . There's so many things in your life that you could never afford. I've wanted to give this to you, but I also wanted to know the perfect timing to do so. Well, that time has come. So, here it is.

"I also have another gift for you. I'm carrying it right here in my pouch." He patted the Chronicle in his pouch. "This one's waiting for you. I'm praying for the moment you ask for it.

"And I'm praying for the moment *you know* . . . it's time."

And he prayed for Zoe.

. . .

The Problem Solver stood up.

And left the room.

Thursday. Midnight. 12:00 a.m.

The group was still there. Norm was on a sofa that had been brought to sit outside Zoe's room. He leaned against Tempie, who leaned against Nick, who leaned against Harold.

Norm's eyes opened and shut depending on the slightest sound.

And then he heard a sound that he recognized. Walking. And he opened his eyes, and way down the hall he saw a person and two kids walking his way. He saw their shadows. And he tried to straighten up.

The lights in the hallways had long ago been dimmed, but he saw the shadows come closer. Then he recognized the shadows.

Norm stood up. His wife was there. And his two children. Becky Adams looked her husband in his eyes under the dimmed lights. And she hugged him. And he hugged back. And his two kids hugged their father's legs. He picked them up and hugged them harder.

"I was in bed. Sleeping," said Becky. "And I was startled awake. I was scared. I knew I was supposed to find you. I had to wake the kids and bring them. I couldn't leave them. I called around. And, I was told to come here. A hospital."

Becky looked at the group as Tempie, Nick, and Harold, shook themselves a little more alive and awake.

Becky looked at Norm. "Look, I don't know why you are here." She looked at the group. "I don't know who these people are." She looked some more. "But I know something . . .

"It's good, whatever it is." And she hugged her husband.

Norm looked at Becky. "I'm so sorry. So, so sorry for everything." And he cried. And they hugged. And the sleepy kids hugged them.

Becky looked into Norm's eyes.
"You've changed."
. . .

Bentley burst out of Zoe's room.
"Doctor!
"Doctor!" he yelled.
"Nurse!!"

T+

19.

Release My Soul . . . part 1

Friday morning. 3:00 a.m.

Zoe Singer woke up . . . on a Friday morning, 3:00 a.m., in early June. Her eyes opened slowly.
Norm Adams was there.
So was the Problem Solver.
So was Bentley.
Everyone else was outside her room. Becky Adams was there, too, on the sofa, asleep. She leaned against Tempie Teagarden, who leaned against Nick Tate, who leaned against Harold Rosenberg . . . in a business suit. Tikipas was vigilant.
. . .

"Hi." Zoe was looking up. Tears were flowing. Norm, Bentley, and the Problem Solver were right there for her.
"Hi," Norm Adams said softly.
The Problem Solver leaned over so Zoe knew he was there. So did Bentley.

"I was dreaming," Zoe said. Her tears were just streaming now.
"You're still with us, Zoe . . . we're here for you," Norm said.
"I have to tell you . . ." she started crying. "Why? . . . I just don't understand, why?"

. . . "Why what?" Norm tried to say.

"Why?" said Zoe.

. . .

"TPS, you there?" Zoe searched those who were looking at her.

"I'm here," he said.

Zoe turned her head slightly to look at the Problem Solver.

"I was dreaming," said Zoe. "What does it mean?" she asked.

"What does what mean?" the Problem Solver asked as quietly as he could.

"I tried so hard, to let go . . . I didn't want to live. I've never really wanted to live." Zoe tried to shift in her bed. She couldn't.

"I dreamed . . . I asked God to give ear to this horrible groaning in my spirit—to just let me go. I didn't want to come back.

"He said . . ." Zoe choked. "He was going . . . to release my soul." She looked at the Problem Solver.

The Problem Solver smiled. And then he had tears. . . . "Those will be the most beautiful words you will ever hear. I promise you."

. . .

"But what does it mean?" Zoe implored the Problem Solver.

"Zoe, the Lord has heeded . . . the crying in your heart. He's heard you."

Zoe turned her head to look up.

"I'm ready . . ."

She looked at the Problem Solver. "Can I have my Chronicle?"

"Yes," I have it right here. The Problem Solver pulled the Chronicle from his pouch. He handed it to her. It was fresh. Zoe could smell the leather cover. She held it over her head.

"It's *time*. It's *time* to fill in my name. It's time to start. I'm going to do it."

Norm, the Problem Solver, and Bentley help Zoe get into position to write her name on her Chronicle.

The Problem Solver handed her his pen.

The pen.

Zoe took three deep breaths. And she wrote her name down.

And showed it to Norm, the Problem Solver, and Bentley. They all looked at it.

1st Chronicle
The life and future of <u>*Baby Doe 1*</u>*.*

Norm didn't understand.

The Problem Solver did.

. . . And, so did Bentley.

"I was wondering, could you all leave me alone for a moment? I think I need . . . a counseling session."

"Yes," said the Problem Solver.

"Yes," said Norm Adams.

"Will you be alright?" Bentley asked, plaintively.

"Bentley," Zoe nodded. ". . . I will be just fine. I just need some time here. *Release my soul.* There are just no words . . ."

"Let's give her some time," said the Problem Solver.

And slowly, Norm, the Problem Solver, and Bentley left Zoe's hospital room.

They shut the door.

And gathered the others.

. . .

T+

20.

Release My Soul . . . part 2

Thirty minutes later. Friday morning. 3:30 a.m.

Zoe Singer sat up in her hospital bed.
She was alone. Physically.
She shifted in her bed, looked for her journal, and found it.
She then sat it next to her new Chronicle.
She picked up her journal. "Good-bye, my old friend." She
kissed it.

She opened her Chronicle. And wrote.
This is what she wrote:

June 8, Friday
Baby Doe 1
Release my soul

Counseling session 1, with the Lord.

This is the first sentence.
And, so I begin. Here I am.
I was hoping to die, but it just didn't work out.

Lord, if you exist, add me to the list of people who don't
believe in you. Why should I believe in you? Where have you
been all my life?

It will take me forever to write this story. I'm not finished putting down all my pain.

I was a trash baby.

Discovered in a dumpster behind a supermarket on Sunset Boulevard. That's me. That's my beginning.

And where were you Lord, assuming you even exist? WHERE WERE YOU!

Then foster home after foster home until I was eighteen. My foster brothers and sisters teased me endlessly. "Baby Doe 1, Baby Doe 1," they would shout at me. And there it was — on my birth certificate.

Baby Doe 1.

Not even typed. It was scrawled.

. . . Who wrote my little name?

Where were you, god? What were you up to, at the time? Busy, I guess.

And then I turned eighteen. And the system turned me out on the street again. No one wanted me, again.

That was ten years ago. *One day* was ten years.

No wonder I was old enough to die.

I had so many names growing up, I can't even remember them.

Baby Doe 1, is the only name I remember. What a name? It's meaningless. It doesn't mean a thing. I'm worthless trash. Thrown away by a mother I will never meet.

Why, god? Why would she just throw me away?

You know, I've been back to that dumpster many times over the years. I see the filth in there. I figure the dumpster's been replaced three times, or just shifted out. I don't know.

New dumpster. Same trash. And me, at one time. I imagine myself in there among the trash.

I spent my life figuring that's where I belong. I wasn't wanted elsewhere either. What did it matter?

And, where were you? What were you up to?

I told my friends I had been going to the Problem Solver for one year. I lied. It's been two years. He's been asking me to do this. Have a counseling session with you. Someone, something, some god, I don't even believe in. What are you, anyway? And where have you been!!

And do I really have friends, anyway? No one's ever cared? I've been in the hospital many times. Even this hospital. And who are these people who have watched over me? No one ever has before.

. . .

God, I have to tell you something, assuming you exist. I love these people. I don't even know them. Really, anyway. I really love them. I'm just so sad, because, I've never felt this thing.
 Love. I feel this . . . somewhere inside.
 I've only known hate. I hate my foster brothers and sisters. I really hate them. What am I to do with that hate? Where do I put it? Store it up? I remember them. I see them. Nagging me. Hitting me. *Baby Doe 1, Baby Doe 1.*

Maybe it's time to stop writing. — But, I do have to deal with this new thing in my heart. Love.
 . . . god, if you exist, thank you for my friends. Why are they nice to me? I love Nick, Harold, Tempie, and Norm. I hardly know them.
 . . . god, did you send them to me?
 Doesn't matter either way, I just love them, or whatever this feeling is.

So, where do I go from here? What do you want with me? I thought I was sick. I thought it was over.
 "Zoe."
 Okay, I wrote that down, but I didn't really hear that. Maybe somewhere in my soul.
 My soul. If I have one, what a beaten, broken, seared, wasted, mangled soul it is. If I have one.
 And, by the way, I'm giving it up. The name "Zoe Singer." I made it up. I tried to get a little life in me, by calling myself

"Zoe." Then I tried to put a song in my step by giving myself a last name, "Singer." I made that up, too.

I can't sing. And my life has been anything but a song.

Maybe I should have called myself "Dead Trainwreck." That would have worked. That's honest.

. . . god, assuming you exist. I'm changing my name back. "Baby Doe 1." I'm okay with it now. It was my name from the beginning, and it will be my name going forward. I kind of like it. It fits me.

So now what? Where do I go from here? Am I really going to live? And if so, why?

"Baby Doe 1."

Yes, Lord. Assuming you exist.

"I do exist. I Am here."

Well, that's interesting. I admit, I basically hear you deep inside my heart. My first desire is to just yell at you.

. . . I just tried. I tried to get my yell going. Nothing came. My body was going to die. I'm assuming my spirit would have died, too, if I had one. My *soul*, do I really have one?

"Yes. . . . Dear Baby Doe 1, I want to talk to you for a moment. Would you consider listening and writing down what I tell you?

. . .

"Would you consider that?"

Okay.

"In your dream, your precious dream, I told you I am going to release your soul. What that means, is that I've heard the groaning in your spirit, the crying in your heart, and I Am going to heal you. I Am going to release your soul to really know Me, and My love for you. *You shall know and feel My strong presence the rest of your life.* And you will know how much I love you. And how I have always been there for you. That I was there the day that Bentley found you in the dumpster."

BENTLEY??
"Yes, Bentley. You were one day old and you saved his life."
Me?
"Yes, you. You gave Bentley, a man with no home, something to live for."

That explains so much.

"So, stand up. My Plan is perfect for you. You will be doing so much more in your life, you can't even imagine. Your life will be abundant and overflowing. I have set divine appointments for you.
"The story of your past will not be the story of your future.
. . .

"Baby Doe 1, you are going to fall in love, you shall marry, and you will have children. You are the new generation of your lineage. And I will bless you.
. . .

"Baby Doe 1, I love you. You are My child. I Am with you, always. I will guide you and protect you.
"Now — stand up! Make your bed. You shall not return to it.
"Ring the nurse and ask for something to eat.
"Go, tell your friends you are going to live.
"Encourage them.
"Then, come back to your room, and open the present Daniel gave you."
Daniel?
"Yes, the Problem Solver. Open the present he gave you. I'm calling you to be a great photographer. Your first showing will be in *one* year.
"And the first topic, 'forgiveness.'
"Black and white photos. And, only one in color.
"Now, go.
"And know, surely I Am coming, *quickly*.

"Indeed, I Am . . .
"here now."
. . .

End of counseling session 1, with the Lord.

Baby Doe 1 finished her writing.
And stood up. She gathered herself. And took a step, and then another.
And then another.
She made her bed.

She opened the door to her hospital room.
And there they were:

The Actor, Nick Tate.
The Professional Man, Harold Rosenberg.
The Everyday Woman, Tempie Teagarden.
The Young Man, Norm Adams.
The Old Farmer, Tikipas.
The Problem Solver.
And, Bentley.

Baby Doe 1 looked at her friends.
"I love all of you so much. So, so much.
"I have a little news for you . . .

"I'm going to live. *Really* live.

"Now, I have a present to open from TPS. And I'm going to eat something. Then I'm packing, and I'm leaving. I'm going to live at the Outreach Center. They invited me.
"And, I'm going to accept.
"I've always wanted a home.

"I think I found one."

T+

PART III

The Abundant Life

21.

When the Morning Comes

Monday morning. 8:30 a.m.
The old courthouse cafeteria, ninth floor.

"We have never seen anything like this!" said Norm Adams. He was sitting across from the Problem Solver.

"You shall see greater things than that," said the Problem Solver.

Norm sat forward.

. . . "Baby Doe 1, just got up and walked out of the hospital Friday morning. *Perfect*. And Saturday, you couldn't slow her down at the Outreach Center. Running around—taking pictures . . . with the camera you gave her. And poor Bentley, he still watches over her—but he couldn't keep up. He borrowed her old wheelchair."

"She won't be needing it anymore," said the Problem Solver.

"No, I guess not. . . .

"And, this weekend, I just fell, completely back in love with my wife. How did I miss . . . all she was to me? How did I miss that . . . until now?"

"We, all of us, are so limited on our own. Especially on our own strength. It's such hard work on our own."

"Why not get God on our side sooner?" asked Norm.

"Well, with God, He'll take any 'soon' you give Him, that's His style," said the Problem Solver. "We are but a mist in this life, and then we're gone. His main concern is eternity."

"I know. But now I know just how much He has for us now. Right now, right here," said Norm.

"You have a strong calling, Norm," said the Problem Solver. "You have the great gift of leadership. This morning, I'm asking you for something."

"Anything," said Norm.

"I'm asking you to be the leader of your group. Pray for them. Work with them. Be there for them. Lead them. Keep them together. Say nothing of me telling you this. Just lead. Will you do that for me?"

"Yes," said Norm.

"Over the next year, your group will experience great blessings and triumphs. But not without challenges. *Prayer*, mostly, will be the answer. Strive toward one hundred counseling sessions with the Counselor. Record each one in your Chronicle. Listen to God. You will know what to do. And, when the answer is not clear, just *stand*, the answer will come. Be patient.

"Remember, do everything on the Lord's strength, be ruthlessly honest with yourself, pray, and surrender.

"Norm, I'm calling you to bring them home."

Norm looked the Problem Solver in the eye.

"I will."

The Problem Solver smiled softly.

"Thank you."

"Now, a few other things. I'd like you to serve as Intern Two all year with me on Saturdays at the Outreach Center, with your prayer partner, Tikipas. Will you do that?"

"Yes."

"Okay, then I release you from the Monday and Friday counseling sessions."

Norm nodded. "Okay." Norm noticed how long both lines were.

"You know, I don't feel like I did much counseling at all," Norm said.

"Precisely," said the Problem Solver. "You're not there to counsel them, you're there to fellowship with them. You do that quite well.

"Also, Becky's birthday is coming. Take her shopping. Buy her whatever she needs, a new sewing machine, fabrics, anything. Becky likes to bless people. Her tablecloths will be a great blessing to many people. Miracles will occur on the tablecloths she designs and gives away or sells. People everywhere will come to know the blessings that come with those tablecloths."

"How did you know?" Norm asked.

"The tablecloths are blue, aren't they?" asked the Problem Solver.

"Yes. They're a deep blue."

"Numbers 4:7 . . . 'Over the table of the Presence they are to spread a blue cloth. . . .' Miracles will occur over those tablecloths."

"I remember now, the words on the tablecloth on our kitchen table. I'm stunned . . ." Norm sat back.

"Norm, take her shopping. That's a blessing that just can't be contained anymore. *The Presence* tablecloth is just one of many she will design. But, *The Presence* will be known. Pray over those tablecloths before they are sent forth."

Norm looked at the Problem Solver. "I will."

"The tables of the righteous shall be blessed."

"One last thing," said the Problem Solver. "Next Saturday, after the morning counseling sessions at the Outreach Center, gather your group at 3:00 p.m. in the Outreach Center War Room. We're going to have a joint counseling session. Will you do that?"

"Yes."

"Good. I will see you next Saturday at 9:00 a.m. at the Outreach Center," said the Problem Solver.

"I'll be there," said Norm.

They both stood up. And hugged.

And Norm Adams started to slowly leave the ninth floor cafeteria. And then, he stopped.

And that was the moment, that he remembered the *moment*, that he first heard the Lord speak to him in his heart. The Lord said to him, *never forget this moment, I shall remind you.*

It was Norm that decided to knock. It was Norm who decided, he wasn't going to drive away. Which led to his first counseling session with the Lord.

That's when it all changed, he thought.

Norm straightened himself up.

I shall never return to that old Norm, he thought.

He looked up.
He spoke out loud.
"Thank You, Lord.
"I'm ready.
"Send me."
. . .

And he walked out of the cafeteria.
Went down the elevator.
And left the courthouse.

And started making telephone calls.
To the group, about next Saturday.

And the upcoming joint counseling session.

T+

22.

The 100th Counseling Session

Tuesday morning. 3:00 a.m.

Nick Tate sat at his writer's desk. The desk looked out over the city. It was 3:00 a.m., it was quiet, but he could still hear the noises of the city.

. . .

He paced.
He took out his Chronicle.
He looked at the cover.

1st Chronicle
The life and future of <u>Nick Tate</u>.

And he wrote.
This is what he wrote:

<u>Counseling session 100, with the Lord.</u>

Lord, it's Nick Tate. I'm here. I made it . . . to my 100th counseling session. You told me, if I could make it to my 100th session, I would stay off of heroin, crack, meth, all the various drugs I took.

Lord, I'm so humbled. I made it. I'm here. I haven't taken any drugs, nothing, for one hundred counseling sessions. I made it.

Lord, why do I feel so dry?

This morning, I look out over the city, and, well, I have to admit, I feel empty. It hurts for some reason. I thought I'd be more, well, ecstatic. Happy. Something. I suppose the weight of all the time I wasted being a drug addict. Me, a drug addict. That's what defined me. Yes, I know I'm sober now, but I feel like I'm still — that drug addict. That *drug addict*. My life was supposed to end badly.

In an alley, behind a building, in an abandoned warehouse, during a crime. Shot, wasted, strung out, beaten, dead.

Instead, I'm here. I'm still standing. I'm alive.

But, I still have to admit.

I feel dry.

You know Lord, I got up at 3:00 a.m. to "celebrate" my 100th counseling session with You.

But — *You know*, I paced around for two hours. Two hours. Actually, the sun is coming up. Well, at least I see the signs. It's getting a little light out there. I can see the outlines of clouds. The outlines of the high-rises. So, I paced for two hours and forty-six minutes.

Why?

Because I feel dry inside.

Is this normal?

I just realized something. Well, I'm not honoring the counseling session. The "counseling" part. The part where I "honor" this time with You. I'm pacing. I know what's going on. "Me."

"I'm" going on. It's "me."

Maybe, it's the last gasp. "Me" is fighting back. "I" want back in. Let me me me me me me me back in. "I, I, I" want back in.

I'm fighting back. I want back in. I want, I want, I want, I want. Can't "I" get back in here?

My body is screaming at me. "I" want everything back. I know what my problem is.

It's my last gasp. It's "my" last gasp.

One Hundredth counseling session. This is it. Exactly what I've been striving for—for a year. A whole year. It took me that long to get here. I had a goal. I made it. I'm here. Sober. *AND DRY.* Dry, dry, dry. Why???

"I" want back in. I want to take over again.

I gave You a year. A whole year. I want back in. I want a hit. My body is screaming at me. It would feel so good.

I know what happened.

I started this session. But I didn't commit to it.

I didn't set my timer. Normally, I set my timer for fifty minutes. I didn't do it this time. Why didn't I? What happened?

Okay, I get it. I didn't set the timer.

I didn't honor this session with You.

What an idiot.

Okay, Lord. Can I start over?

Here I go. I will set my timer for fifty minutes. Lord, I will honor this next fifty minutes with You. I will honor that time. So, hold on for just a sec, and I will set my timer.

. . .

Fifty minutes. Go. I'm ready.

Okay, Lord, thanks for letting me start over. Timer is set, and the session has started.

Lord, thank You so much for the last ninety-nine counseling sessions with You! I made it! I'm here. I'm ALIVE.

Alive. Wow, what it means to be alive, when I know that I definitely would have been dead by now.

So, I'm here.

Lord, I'm so sorry for those moments when I want to take back over. I don't know what happens to me.

But, I really hate that dry feeling. It's horrible.

Father God, thank You. I made it 100 sessions. Thank You.

Lord, help me with a Plan for the future. I realize that making it to this 100th session was really all I thought about last year, and doing exactly what You told me to do, session by session. So, now I'm here. Oh my, I'm so thankful. So, now what? Where do I go from here?

I feel so alive inside, what is this?

Real quick, can I get some coffee? I have forty-three minutes left in this session and I'd really like to have a cup of coffee with You, and see what happens.

"Nick, you can get a cup of coffee, and then, let's talk. You, and Me."

Okay, hold on just a moment.

. . .

Lord, the coffee is brewing, but my head is spinning with the names and faces of all the people I have to thank for making it this far. Lord, TPS, thank You, Lord, for him. And Lord, the group I finally found. It took close to a year to get my group, but I realize just how perfect Your timing is. Thank You for Baby Doe 1, Harold Rosenberg, Tempie Teagarden, and Norm Adams, and all my new friends at the Outreach Center. I'm so blessed.

Well, hold on, the coffee is ready.

. . .

Okay, no excuses. I have my coffee now. But, I only have thirty- two minutes left in the counseling session and I don't want to miss anything.

So, what's next? Where to?

"Nick. It's time. I'm going to bring you the love of your life. You will get married and have children. Five to be exact. Three children with your wife, and you and your wife will adopt two that are introduced to you by the Outreach Center. These children will have been abandoned. And you and your wife will adopt them. And love them."

Lord, I . . . don't know what to say. Well, actually, I do. Yes. I say, yes!

"For now, I want you to serve Tempie Teagarden. She has a dream to start a little café. I want you to help her. I want you to

serve her. Don't tell her I told you this. Just serve her. Whatever she asks of you. Help her."
Yes. Yes, Lord. I will.

"So, we have twenty-five minutes left in our session. What would you like to talk about?"
Lord, sometimes I'm afraid. My cravings come screaming back at me, and I'm afraid I'll fail. I'll break down. I know, stay close to You. Really close. I'm doing pretty good, but it's scary at times.

"Nick, as TPS has told you: Serve until you're healed, and then keep serving to stay healed.

"Nick, I declare: *You are healed*. Now, keep serving to stay healed. Right now, I want you to serve Tempie. You have the gift of hospitality. I want the café to be a place of peace, My peace. A place of encouragement. A place of health. You can help her. She needs help with organization, ordering, planning, budgeting, you can help. Will you help her?"
Yes, of course I will.

"Good, she will ask you. Respond. Don't tell her we've spoken. Just help her."
Okay, Lord. I will.

"Good. Also, I want you to be a server at the café. I want you to encourage everyone you serve. Watch every word you say to the customers. Encourage them. Help them. Pray for them if they ask. I want everyone who comes to the café to be blessed. And, I'm *sending* you. Will you go?"
Yes, yes, of course I will. I'm already looking forward to it.
"Good, do you have any other questions?"

Yes. Father God. I look at all these tattoos on my arms, my body. They sometimes bring back bad memories. I remember where I was at the time. I remember what they symbolized. They're permanent. Now what?
"Nick, your body is now the temple of the Holy Spirit.
"You are *filled* with the Holy Spirit.
"You have been healed.

"The story of your past is a strong part of the story of your future.

"Many will know from where you came, and many will trust you for it.

"My message, through you, will be even stronger.

"You are My letter, written not with ink but with the Spirit of the living God, not on tablets of stone but on tablets of human hearts.

"Remember . . . I chose you.

"Do you have any other questions?"

. . .

I guess I want to ask You when I'm going to find the love of my life, but I have a feeling I have to wait on that?

"Nick, I love you. You have an incredible future ahead of you. Stay close to Me. And remember, I'm always with you. Always.

"Now, go. I want you to spend the last few minutes of this session in prayer. Be at peace.

"Be ready.

"And, pray."

Okay, I will.

Amen.

And, amen.

End of counseling session 100, with the Lord.

T+

23.

Anno Domini

June 16, Saturday afternoon. 3:00 p.m.

"We shall not fear.
"We shall not tarry.
"We shall not hesitate.
"We are called to be bold!
"We shall record everything the Lord lays on our heart for the next fifty minutes.
"Everything.

"When the timer starts, you start. You know in your heart you are to listen and write. Don't question. Lean not on your own understanding.
"This is start day.
"Anno Domini."

"You are now together. You have found yourselves. But what you've found is just the start. I'm looking at a powerful prayer team. A powerful family. Miracles, each one of you. Brought together. But why? Well, let's ask Him. Let's go to the throne room.

"Ask, and it will be given to you.
"Knock, and the door will be opened to you.

"One year is a very precious amount of time. This is the year of our Lord. And, in this year of our Lord, this is also, *your* year. You shall be uplifted, you shall be renewed, you shall fight, you shall overcome, you shall shine. And, you shall never . . . be the same.

"The only path that matters is the one that led you here.

"I declare that you *are ready*, and to the extent you don't feel ready, that's okay, you shall be even more ready, more open to . . . *listen.*

"I promise that the Lord has a powerful message for each of you. Receive it.

"This is your start day of a one-year journey."

The Problem Solver stopped and looked at the group.

There they were. Poised over their respective Chronicles. Quiet.

The Young Woman, Baby Doe 1.
The Actor, Nick Tate.
The Professional Man, Harold Rosenberg.
The Everyday Woman, Tempie Teagarden.
And the Young Man, Norm Adams.

"I brought two friends to be with us."
Just then Tikipas and Bentley walked in.
"Two prayer warriors. The three of us will be here with you during this counseling session.

"You are ready."

One by one, everyone said:
"Yes."

"Okay, it is 3:05 p.m. . . . *Go!*"
The Problem Solver's timer can be seen by all.

Within a few moments, they all start to write.

This is what Tempie Teagarden wrote:

June 16, Saturday
Tempie Teagarden
Café Heaven

Counseling session 1, with the Lord.

There's only one reason I want to do this. There's only one reason I'm open to this.

Love. I have a secret. A secret love. And, down deep I'm happy. Lord, if you exist, and if I'm to find out your plan for me, that's fine. But only because I have a secret love. I've never had this before, so,

I shall carry on.

And, if you have a plan for me. I'm listening. I'm open, for the next 46:37 minutes.

I'll hear you out.

"Tempie,"

Yes, I'm here. But you know that.

"In one year, you are going to open an amazing café. *Inspired*, with Me as your Counselor. I will guide you.

"I'm calling you to complete One Hundred counseling sessions just like this. Will you do that?"

Lord, is that you talking in my heart? Where are you?

"I'm here with you. It is Me."

Okay, well, it doesn't matter either way. There's no harm in writing this all down. How can I go wrong? I see my friends, Harold, Baby Doe 1, Norm, and Nick writing away. They seem so inspired. Should I be that inspired also?

"Tempie, just write. Okay?"

Yes.

41:41 minutes left to go. I'm still rolling. Slowly.

I feel TPS's hands on my shoulders. So, I'll write that down. But other than that . . .

And my heart picks up. What's that? I feel Bentley's hand on my head. Softly. I hear their prayers. Okay, fine I'll write that down. It gives me something to write. I'll just push ahead. Push ahead. Slowly, I'm not afraid to write. I can live this through. One sentence at a time. What's the big deal? There's nothing to fear in that.

I just wish I didn't feel this relief. This peace. I'm not used to this. Take it away. Give me the familiar. Give me the peace of familiarity. The peace of arrogance. I'm fine the way I am.

What's that shooting through me? Wow! What's that?

"Tempie, you are not your mind. Turn your mind off. Turn it off."

My mind is all I have.

"No, you are spirit, you have a soul, and you live in a body. You — are spirit. And I'm talking to your spirit. Write that down. Write down only what your spirit is telling you. That's it. Turn your head off, turn your mind — off."

Okay! Here goes:

Oh, that is nice. I have to admit that. Oh! That is nice. Oh! Can I stay here for a while? I feel like I just sailed away. Oh! That is nice. Lord, this is nice. Mind!! — turn off. Stay turned off. I see my mind over there.

Just churning.

The vortex. Oh myyyyy! I see such torment. I've savaged my mind.

Oh my! What a vision. *It's me.* Looking at my mind and how it works.

How it works against me. I never knew how to use it.

So . . . who is this "me" looking at my mind? It's not my mind. So, who is this me?

"Tempie, you are spirit."

I see my mind as a tool that I've never used correctly. My mind is not me. It is not me. It's just a tool. Part of my soul.

I truly am *spirit.*

Me . . . how are you? You're not all bad. I like this. I feel I'm meeting . . . the real *me.* Who is this me? Not all bad.

Now I feel Tikipas' hands on my shoulders. Wow! What power. I just feel his strength, and courage, and peace running through me. His spirit is so strong, so centered. I want that, Lord. I want that.

Oh mercy, what is that? I can't put that into words. Thank You! Lord. Thank You.

My spirit is all good. It has nothing but love. I feel it. Lord, I have so much to give. What is this spirit? What is this *me*?

"Tempie, it is you. You are a beautiful person. Whole and complete in Me. And wholly communicating with Me. My Holy Spirit is communicating with your precious spirit. So, keep writing. Record all of this."

I'm writing. I'm writing.

"One year from today. Saturday. June 15, 8:00 a.m. you will open your café. *Café Heaven*. On that morning, you will complete your One Hundredth counseling session with Me. I will have guided you the entire way. And, you will have lots of help.

"First, ask Norm for help. He will help with financing, a business plan, and logistics. His wife will help in a very special way. You don't need to know that now.

"Second, ask Baby Doe 1 for help. She will help with many aspects of the design, the settings, and decorating. Her photography will be part of setting the tone for the café. And, she will have her first public opening at your café that first afternoon, starting at 2:00 p.m. It shall be a glorious event. Very healing, very appointed.

"Third, ask Harold to help. Ask him now, in the next week. He will help in many ways, but his music will also set the tone for the café. His music is his great gift, and he will play the first day the café opens. I'm also asking you to do something special for Harold, six months from now. Six months from now, call him up and remind him of his great gift, his *charisma*. Implore him with much urgency that he continue to receive this gift for the rest of his life. That he share it with the saints, and all who will listen. The call from you will surprise him. And he will understand that he is a partaker of the heavenly calling.

"Fourth, ask Tikipas. He will be the main cook. He's very gifted.

"Fifth, ask Bentley. He will have divine appointments and assignments to attend to, and he shall.

"And, ask the love of your life, Nick Tate, for help. He will be with you the whole way."

Nick?

"Yes, Nick."

Lord, *You know.* I fell for him that day he came over and we baked 200 muffins. *200!!* I guess I would have baked anything that day. That was the most beautiful day in my life. I know I shouldn't expect him to like me.

Am I cute enough?

Am I not the right age?

Am I ugly, Lord? I can ask You, can't I?

Lord, I know all this depression has aged me. I simply don't look good. I'm not pretty. I'm not . . . sexy. I'm not lovable.

"Tempie, I Am healing you. The dew of your youth is with you. Nick is perfect for you. Don't worry about how he sees you.

"Receive My healing. Receive My love. Stay close to Me for this year. Will you do that?"

Yes, Yes! Yes, of course.

"Okay, I'm giving you the final blessing for this session.

"Know that I Am with you always."

I just heard TPS say time's up. Oh no, I don't want to stop. I want more time. I don't want to stop.

"Tempie, tomorrow morning when you get up, come to your Chronicle and let's have your second counseling session.

"Will you do that?"

Yes, I will. I'll be there.

Thank You, Lord.

Amen.

End of counseling session 1, with the Lord.

T+

Six months later

24.

It's Never Darkest before the Dawn

When the principalities assemble—they don't send out an alert. They never will. You can pick it up in your spirit sometimes, but it is you who better be on the alert.

It can happen at any time.

December 14, Friday night. 6:00 p.m.

Norm Adams and his wife Becky, and their two kids had just sat down for dinner when there was a knock on the door.

Becky, with a hop to her step, ran to the door to open it.

Beauty can be ramped up. And the girl from Chelsea's had done her best in that regard.

"Hi, I'm Norm's girlfriend, from Chelsea's. We haven't seen him in a while. So, I took matters into my own hands. Is Norm home? Tell him it's his girlfriend. I miss him." And, with confidence, her chin and chest puffed up.

And Norm, sitting at the kitchen table, heard a voice he thought he had left behind.

And, at the Outreach Center, Baby Doe 1, was primping herself in the mirror, it had been an exciting day. She was six months away from an amazing goal to have her first opening as a photographer. Her first showing would be *"Forgiveness."* And so much was still pouring out of her.

She ran her hands down the side of her face. Her skin was smooth. As her hands slid under her jaw and to her neck, she felt it. A lump.

She had never felt that before.

She screamed. Her first jolt of reaction scared her. So on edge. And the memories came screaming back at her.

The dumpster. The hittings from her siblings. The abandonment on the street. No love. All hate. All meanness. All aloneness. All the hunger. Horrible health. All the blankness of worthless existence.

And she collapsed on the floor.

If she could tighten enough into a ball, she could be done now.

And, uptown, Harold was in his living room. He was played out. He was finished. Everything he had felt had been played out on his harp. He hit a horrible empty beat-up dry dry dry zone.

And what was he doing anyway? At his age. A middle-aged man thinking he could relive his youth as a musician. What was he thinking? This was stupid. His whole professional world thought he was stupid. Playing the harp again. *How quaint? How cute*, was the best response he received from his professional world. Whatever cut into his productivity at work was never worth the price in his world.

He needed to take up golf. That's what his friends suggested.

He even had a wife. Shirley. She was lukewarm at best to this new Harold who had developed over the last six months. What was this all about? Just a phase.

She decided to wait it out. It, too, would pass. It wasn't so bad anyway. It gave her more time on the tennis court.

Harold sat down on his living room sofa.

And he sunk back. And back. And back. He was mad. Time had passed him by. His dreams were dead.

He jumped up. His head was racing. His mind was slammed.

Enough.

He pushed his harp over.

And it crashed to the floor.

And, downtown, in a little apartment sat Nick Tate. And he sat. This acting thing wasn't going to work out. He had to be honest with himself. He hadn't gone to an audition or a go-see in, well, so long he couldn't remember. He looked at his glossies. Such a rugged guy-look thing going on. Didn't a producer need a tough, hard, rock-solid, nothing can hurt him, bad to the bone loner, don't-care guy for his next film? *Hollywood's paved with guys like me,* he thought. The look is really, underemployed, looking, and looking, with no hope in sight.

And what girl would want him anyway? No real job, no future. Nothing going on. Wasted. Sober. But still wasted. And not much different.

And the thoughts rolled through.

Loneliness.

He thought about Tempie.

Oh, she's just a friend, he thought. She had gotten prettier over the last six months. So determined to open her café. But that was her goal. What about me? How did I fit in? And now she's cute? No hope for me. What is she anyway? A friend. More like a comfortable old blanket.

It's time I told her I need to move on. I can't help her anymore. I'm going home. She doesn't need to know I don't have a home.

Just a new city. That's all I need.

Colorado sounds good. Boulder. I'll head up there.

But first I'll make the call.

Time to tell her I'm done.

Enough.

He's going to call her. Call Tempie. It's done.

As soon as he gets the strength to do it. He's tough.

He can do it.

Time to quit.

And, across town, Tempie Teagarden stopped at her mailbox before walking upstairs to her little studio apartment. She gathered her mail, headed upstairs, and went inside. In the stack of mail there were brochures on design, restaurant design, coffee shops, tea, creative foods, art, decorating, mixed in with bills, notes, and a letter from the city. Oh, she thought, *what's this?*

She opened the letter.

Her eyes saw it all. Really just one paragraph.

And she saw a word toward the end of the paragraph.

Denied.

Denied, what? So soon? What happened? And she melted toward the floor.

Nick had found the perfect spot for her café. An old warehouse. It was big. Cavernous. Lots of space. She would need it. It had such potential.

Her mind raced through the letter again.

Plumbing too old.

Fire-life-safety issues.

Old paint. "Old paint?!" she screamed.

She was on the floor. She looked up at her walls. Covered with huge pieces of art paper with designs, layouts, color combinations, lists, lists, lists,

and she's six months away from opening, oh, but

nowhere to open.

Her first idea.

Pills. They always fixed depression in the past,

and now she needed them

more, more than ever . . .

It's always darkest before the dawn. Clichés, can be helpful on occasion. But so wrong.

It's never darkest before the dawn.

It's darkest at the halfway point. The darkest place at night is 180 degrees from the sun. It is darkest at midnight. It is darkest at the time which is the midpoint from dusk to dawn.

Even if you've climbed the mountain, you still have to return. It's on the return that most of the deaths occur.

When the principalities gather. They can be strong.

But, not strong enough.

Unless . . . you let them.

. . .

T+

25.

I Love You

December 14, Friday night. 9:00 p.m.

Nick Tate had summoned his strength. And he dialed the number. On the oldest phone still in existence.

And Tempie Teagarden picked up, on the last ring, because none remained.

"Hello," the voice was faint. But it was Tempie.
"Tempie, it's Nick.
"Look, I don't know how to tell you this, but I'm done.
"I can't help you anymore.
"I'm done.
"I'm leaving. I'm finished. It was nice, but I have to move on. I can't do this anymore.
"Tempie, do you hear me?" Nick said with firm, measured syllables.
. . .

"Tempie, do you hear me?"
"Yes," she said. A word can be empty. Yet heard.
"Well . . . I'm leaving. Tomorrow I'm done with this city. Enough. I'm ready. New city. New life.
"I'm sorry. Well, I just wanted to tell you."
. . .

"I understand. I totally understand . . ." Tempie sat up as best she could. She also had a little strength left. One last thought had to be expressed. Down deep, it welled up.

She tried to clear her passages. She sniffed, and took a deep breath . . . suddenly she felt so sure.

So sure.

"Nick, I just have one last thing to tell you.

"I'm sorry I waited so long, but it just doesn't matter anymore. It just doesn't matter.

. . .

"I love you Nick Tate. I've loved you since that day we baked 200 muffins together.

"That will be the best day ever in my life.

"Nick Tate, I love you. I love you. I love you.

"I love you so much

"and if these are my last words, so be it.

"I love you, I love you,

"and it doesn't matter, because I've swallowed enough pills to sink a battleship. And I ain't no battleship. So,

"I love you, I love you, I LOVE YOU.

"And i, yes, i, the smallest little *nothin'* . . . will never, ever, never, ever forget you,

"but it doesn't matter anymore . . .

"I   love   you . . ."

"Tempie!!" Nick shouted into the phone.

But it went dead.

. . .

T+

26.

The Complacency of Fools

December 14, Friday night. 11:00 p.m.

Norm Adams pounded through the hospital door.
He ran. The hallway was long.
All Norm could hear as he ran down the hall were the words:
"What happened here?" A nurse was yelling at Nick Tate, Baby Doe 1, and Harold Rosenberg.
"What happened here? — This girl tried to take her life. What happened? *I want to know!*" She was throwing things. Towels. Plastic cups. Her weight. "Look, I don't know her. But you do! I want to know — WHAT HAPPENED HERE!"
"I let her down," said Nick. Yelling, "I LET HER DOWN. That's what happened here. I let her down. It's Friday night, I should have been with her. But, I wasn't. I was wallowing in stupid, disgusting, self- pity. This is my fault! I should have been there."
The nurse turned on Nick:
"Well, I'm telling you right now, the doctors are in there trying their best to revive her. Pumping her stomach, doing everything they can to bring her back." She slammed some cabinets. "I'm getting sick, sick, sick of seeing this. Why aren't we looking out for each other?? You better all think about this. There is no excuse for this. I'm sick, sick, sick of seeing this."

The nurse looked at everyone in the eye. And in the eye of Norm Adams. "All of you better pray. You don't get it, do you?" The nurse shook her head.

"DO ANY OF YOU LOVE THIS WOMAN? Is there someone here? Hello!!"

The nurse tried her best — to walk off. She turned, abruptly. "Apparently, this woman has people in her life who don't know just how precious she is, how precious life is — how we are *called* to look out for each other."

The nurse looked at:

The Young Woman with the skier's cap.
The Actor with long hair and tattoos.
The Professional Man, in a business suit.
And, the Young Man.

"I'm looking at a bunch of fools. Got all chilled out and comfortable didn't we?" Her eyes blazed at Nick. "Got a little time for self-pity? How nice. Comfy, isn't it?" Then her eyes blazed at all of them.

And they looked back.
And she looked at them.
"You're together for a reason."
And she walked away . . . slowly.

Bentley and Tikipas walked up.
Tikipas surveyed the group.
They stood there in the hallway.
And they prayed.
One by one.

December 15. Saturday morning. 12:30 a.m.

The doctor came down the hall to talk to the group. He looked at the group.

He was stern. "I want to know what happened here. Are any of you family?"

"Well, we consider ourselves her family, but we don't know if she has any real family," said Norm.

"You better go through her belongings, because family should be notified. We've checked her purse, but we've found nothing. We called all the numbers on her phone, but they all go to you," said the doctor, and he looked at Nick Tate, Norm Adams, Harold Rosenberg, and Baby Doe 1. "We can't find any other family. Like I said, you better go through her belongings and see if she has family."

And he walked off.

"But how is she?" asked Norm.

The doctor turned. "She's not good . . ." he searched for more words.

. . .

December 15. Saturday morning. 3:00 a.m.

"For the waywardness of the simple will kill them, and the complacency of fools will destroy them."

Norm looked at his friends, Nick Tate, Harold Rosenberg, and Baby Doe 1. Tikipas and Bentley were close by.

"Yesterday at about 6:00 p.m., my wife, my two kids, and I were sitting down to dinner. There was a knock at the door. And Becky, in her usual fashion, bounced up to get it.

"I heard Becky open the door.

"And then I heard the voice of a girl and a life I thought I had left behind. My old girlfriend from Chelsea's. I heard her:

'Hi, I'm Norm's girlfriend. I haven't seen him in a while. So, I took matters into my own hands. Is Norm home? Tell him it's his girlfriend. I miss him.'

"And I could picture her standing there. Pretty as usual. Tall. Sexy. And my heart sunk. I had every right to lose my wife, and my kids, *again*.

"In seconds, I was crushed . . .

"I sat there frozen, at the dinner table . . .

"And, do you know what my wife said?"

Nick, Harold, and Baby Doe 1 waited.

"I heard my wife say: 'I was wondering when you'd show up. What took you so long?

'Are you hungry? We were just sitting down for dinner.'

"And the girl was so flummoxed, she accepted.

"The bottom line is, my wife was never complacent. She was prepared. There's a vigilance about my wife.

"The girl's name is Candice. I used to call her Candy. She ate dinner with us. And I thought about that tablecloth spread under the plates we served her. The Presence. She stayed. And she baked cookies with the kids. And we saw her change. But it was me who changed.

"I should have seen that coming. But, I didn't.

"Becky did."

December 15. Saturday morning. 7:00 a.m.

Harold spoke.

His face was drawn. He stared at the hospital floor.

"I'm forty-seven years old. I have a wife. We don't know each other. I live in a big house, filled with stuff. No kids, and no effort. *And I think I'm going to be a musician again?* We pay a heavy price for the choices we make and the choices we leave behind.

"I have the worst flaw imaginable. I see it. I see its face.

"Trust.

"Why do I have to be this old, to see?

"I chose the safe route."

Harold continued to stare.

Norm, Nick, and Baby Doe 1 just sat close by.

December 15. Saturday afternoon. 3:00 p.m.

Baby Doe 1 spoke.

"I found such comfort in poor health. But now—that I know exactly what I'm supposed to do, I want my comfort back. It's easier. I want it to be easy.

"I want to be sick again.

"Why? Why do I want to be sick again? Can anyone help me with that? I'll never be able to deal with this." And she waves her arms at the world. *"Forgiveness.* What is it, when it eats at you?

"I destroyed my camera yesterday. I didn't just destroy it, I slammed it over and over again onto the floor of my little room, at the Outreach Center. . . . I was thinking of my mom. Someone, I will never meet. Someone who dumped me. And I slammed it, over and over again into the floor. As hard as I could, until it was only my hand."

She looked at Norm, Nick, and Harold. "Will I ever, ever, ever be able . . ."

December 15. Saturday evening. 7:15 p.m.

They heard her.

The nurse.

Norm, Nick, Harold, and Baby Doe 1 heard her as she walked up the hall to them. She would have thrown something, if available.

Still mad. "So I have a little news for you. Ms. Teagarden is stabilized. And, oh, we got ahold of her family. Oh yeah. In upstate New York. The high-rent district." She emphasized the accent. "They said they hadn't seen Tempie in a while. And their hearts and prayers go out to her. THEIR WHAT?! THEIR WHAT?! They ain't got no hearts. And they can take their prayers—" and the nurse kicked over a chair. It had been kicked over before. "Worthless, piece a . . ." She found a cabinet to slam. "That ain't praying. I'm telling you—that ain't praying . . . Oh, and they're a little busy right now. They won't be flying out."

She looked at them: Norm Adams, Nick Tate, Harold Rosenberg, and Baby Doe 1.

"Let me tell each one of you something: abandonment can come in many forms."

She tried to walk off, but couldn't. She turned to them.

Her weight loomed over them, and it wasn't physical.

"Am I looking at a bunch of tools, or am I looking at family? Because that girl needs family. And you—are all she's got."

. . . And the nurse was gone.

The hallway seemed content, knowing she was there. Somewhere.

December 16. Sunday. Midnight. 12:00 a.m.

It's never darkest before the dawn.

It was so dark that night. If there was a moon, dark clouds covered it. And the four sat there. Norm, Harold, Nick, and Baby Doe 1. Outside Tempie's room. Not allowed in. If they even tried they would be thrown out of the hospital. They'd been warned. "You go through that door and I break your arm," said the nurse. "It will snap like a toothpick."

And they suddenly heard her voice. "Now that's some praying. *My kind of praying.*" The nurse was walking down the hall, but she was smiling. "You best all go outside right now — get, get out! Move!! NOW! Go, Go! Get your butts moving!"

Norm, Harold, Nick and Baby Doe 1 walked down the long hall to the front door.

Jonathan was there from the Outreach Center. And perhaps a thousand people. It was quiet. And they were praying. Candles flickered. There was a glow.

Jonathan saw the four walk out. "We'll stay 'til the morning. This is the dark night. But it won't take her. She still has a special thing to do with her life. I know in my heart . . . she will still have that special thing. So join us."

And the four sat down on the sidewalk.

Norm saw the faces of so many people he had gotten to know at the Outreach Center. There's something about pulling for someone that makes you pull for yourself. Over that last six months, well, the family was much larger than Norm estimated. Tempie Teagarden had served approximately 10,000 of her and Nick's muffins over the last six months. And Norm saw their faces. And he saw the messages.

People were actually clinging to the messages that Nick and Tempie had put into the muffin cups. They were pulling for "their" Tempie.

Nick noticed. People had a vise grip on their message, but it was clear in their hand. The night was dark. There was a breeze, and none would be let to slip away.

December 16. Sunday. 9:00 a.m.

Nick Tate spoke.

"I wanted fame.

"I wanted to get lost in the roles other people threw at me. And I'd be good. Everybody'd love me. I'd be cool.

"But when that didn't happen, drugs would take me there.

". . . There was no *there* there.

"I was heading toward drugs no matter what happened."

He looked up at this friends. He sat across from Norm Adams, Harold Rosenberg, and Baby Doe 1.

"Is it just me, or do all of us have a set date and time we're supposed to be at in six months?"

"I do," said Norm.

"I do," said Harold.

"I do," said Baby Doe 1.

"You know what? I'm going to turn my life over to this. I'm done living for myself. Done, finished, *finite*." And Nick Tate was done talking.

"Me too," said Norm.

"Me too," said Harold.

"I'm in," said Baby Doe 1.

The Actor with long hair and tattoos, carefully placed his Chronicle down on the table.

The Young Woman with the skier's cap, carefully placed hers on top of his.

The Professional Man, in a business suit, slowly placed his on top of the others.

And, the Young Man . . . slowly, placed his on top.

December 16. Sunday. 2:00 p.m.

By the daring afternoon of the high reaches of that hospital a subtle breeze began to blow through.

And the nurse was there. "Oh mercy! Oh mercy! Oh mercy!!" And she whisked into Tempie's room.
She was in there for the longest time.
And when she emerged.
She looked at the group. She nodded.
"She's sleeping."
And she looked at each of them. "I now *know* what I'm looking at." And she left them with a warm smile.

December 16. Sunday. 9:00 p.m.

It had crossed their minds, on several occasions. Where was the Problem Solver?
And then he was there. They saw him from a distance walking down the long hallway.
And he sat across from them.

"Does it really matter why you were raised up to do something so much more important, more exciting, more eternal than anything, *anything*, you could come up with?
"But, indeed you were."

December 16, 2013. Sunday. 10:50 p.m.

The doctor emerged from Tempie's room.

"Tempie is awake. She had a good rest today. She's asked for one of you. Which one of you is Nick Tate?"

T+

27.

I Could Have Died without Telling You

December 16, Sunday night. 11:00 p.m.

Nick Tate walked into Tempie Teagarden's room.

Tempie was staring at the ceiling.

"Nick . . . could you sit down for just a second. And let me . . . think."
Nick takes a small chair right by Tempie's bed.

". . . I don't know why I'm here. I don't remember ever making the decision to be here. Alive, and living on this earth. I simply never felt like I was supposed to be here. I felt abandoned. Like I was just left here. Alone. With no directions. With no purpose. No meaning. Nothing.
"I've spent my whole life not wanting to get out of bed. Waking up and not wanting to move. Not willing to swing my little body around to place my feet on the little platform of my bed,
"that is only a foot from the floor.
"That's a . . . long foot to reach the floor.
"So often, I wasn't able to do it, and I just stayed in bed.
"I just figured there was no hope to finding out why I was here, what I was supposed to do here."

"Tempie—" Nick said.
"No, let me finish." Tempie moved her head to face Nick Tate.

"Nick, I'm sorry I told you I love you . . . but, I knew,
". . . I could have died without telling you.
"And telling you I love you, meant something so wonderful to me. Somehow, I knew when I told you that . . . that there was something more than me. The moment I told you . . . I knew I was supposed to live, and yet I had done so much to end my life . . .
"It was too late.

"Nick, what is it about love that makes me want to live. No question intended. I don't really care if you love me back.
"I'm just so glad I found love,
"I feel love,
"there really is a reason to live.
"You know, I don't want to die now,
"somehow my depression has lifted.
"I feel so beat up, so broken, but . . . I am . . . healing.
"I'm going to live.

"I'm going after this thing. Life. Whatever this is. I'm going after it. *Life.* Whatever this is. I'm going after it. I'm going to chase it down, tackle it, embrace it, hug it, and say, hey, you're okay, you're worth it,
"and, I'm going to love."

Nick tries to take Tempie's hand. She pulls back.
"Let me finish. I have more to say to you.
"Nick, I know why I love you.

". . . you're insane,
"what you did was completely insane. You found the biggest, most unlikely spot possible for a coffeehouse. It's huge, it's completely unsafe, there's no fire-life-safety in place, the building will crumble in an earthquake, the plumbing's bad, the neighborhood is unsafe,

"abandoned . . .

"so when the City told me my permit was denied, I was finished. Done. Over.

"Nick, I already knew you were going to leave. I saw it in your eyes. You had lost faith,

"in yourself. You had lost faith *in yourself.* And I figured if you lost faith in yourself, then who am I to have faith in myself,

"so . . . I gave up—

"but, Nick. I've decided not to give up. I'm going to get up. I'm going to march out there into the hall and I'm going to ask my friends,

"I'm going to ask you—to not give up on me.

"I came so close to committing the most disgustingly selfish thing in my life. But, you saved me. And then . . . I knew why.

"Nick, I'm asking you to not give up on me. I'm asking you to not leave. *Stay.*

"I don't really think . . . I'm *nothing* anymore. I am something. You are something.

"Nick. Keep our group together. Please? I love you so much, but it's okay. Just—let me say that to you once in a while. That's all I ask. Nothing else.

"And,

"thank you.

"Now, I need a counseling session. I'm going to hit that number. 100. The Hundredfold. I know for me, that's when the real blessings will kick in. I know I'm supposed to hit that number. I know it. And I will.

"And, I have a café to open in six months,

"and nothing's going to stop me.

"Nothing.

"Please assemble the group. I want to talk to them. I need a counseling session first, but then,

"I need to talk to the group.

"Nick, thank you."

. . .

Nick Tate reached over to Tempie in her bed and hugged her. She hugged back. Then he started to leave.
He turned around and looked at Tempie.

"Tempie, can I tell you just one thing? Just one thing?"

She looked back. "Okay, just one thing."

Nick took a deep breath.
"The group is assembled.
" — And the date and time is set."

And he left the hospital room.
— Quickly.

T+

Relatively close to another six months later

28.

I Read Your Chronicle Last Night

June 8, Saturday night. 9:00 p.m.

Shirley Rosenberg was sitting at a coffeehouse in Silver Lake . . . with her husband.

The coffeehouse was bustling, enchanting, the vibe was clear and clean. In the corner a poet sang her verses while playing her guitar. A guitar refurbished, strung, and repaired on many a Saturday morning at the Outreach Center. The sparrow logo, so little so certain, showing the guitar's upkeep from the Outreach Center.

The attentiveness to her was active, heads moving, call-outs, and smiles. Who was the poet and who was the listener?

Who could write a poem like that, and put it with music. No question intended.

The flow.

Shirley Rosenberg sipped her tea and looked at her husband.

And looked.

"i read your Chronicle last night."

And she looked some more. "i'm sorry i never got to know you. i'm so sorry. And i'm . . ."

Harold reached out: "No, it's okay—"

"No! Let me finish," she said. "Last night i listened to you playing. i listened until i fell asleep. Where could all of that come from? The notes, the movement, the songs, i fell asleep and had the best sleep of my life . . .

"then, i woke up, and you weren't with me. And i missed you so much. i went down to the living room. And there you were sleeping. And i crawled up against you on the floor . . .

"and why, was that the happiest moment of my life? Why? So, i wanted to thank you for including me on this adventure. Whatever *this* is?

"So there i was on the floor, and your music was still in the air. You were so warm and you hugged me back . . .

"and i saw this book by you. Your Chronicle. i was lying on my side and i flipped it open and i read the first page . . .

"and the second . . . and the third. i could hear your music from the pages. i could hear your life from the pages. i was enthralled. i read your whole Chronicle . . .

"and there i was sitting on the floor of our living room, with this big ol' *rented* harp, all the amps, the wires, handwritten notes everywhere, and my husband curled up on the floor asleep . . .

"and i read everything you wrote. and i read everything you said about me. it was all so . . . *positive* . . . so loving. and i understand why you've been bringing me to all these coffeehouses to listen to music, to just be, just be here, and i fought it at first, and something happened to me . . .

"and here we are again. i'm so thankful. What happened? How did this all start? . . . well, i read your Chronicle. And i see it. i'm so sorry i didn't get to know you . . .

"and at the same time so thankful, i'm with you now, right here, right now,

"i just want you to know that last night was the happiest moment of my life,

"and the last six months have been the happiest of my life . . . thank you for including me in all this. i came so close to not being part of this. i came so close to rejecting it . . .

"i just don't want it anymore: comfort and pillows, and rooms, and big houses, and shelves filled with stuff . . .

"So, i was wondering . . . can we sleep on the floor more often?"

And with that, Shirley slowly sipped her tea. And got ahold of herself.

. . . Harold leaned forward, elbows on the table, hands crossed under his chin. "I would never consider walking this life without you, Shirley. I will love you forever. 'Til my last note."

And in the middle of a coffeehouse in Silver Lake, a little town outside of downtown Los Angeles, a middle-aged couple got up and hugged for the longest time.

And the poet saw them.

"Hey everybody, that's Harold Rosenberg. Harold Rosenberg is in the house tonight."

And there was applause.

"Did you bring your harp?"

"No," said Harold. "I brought the love of my life."

And everyone applauded again.

"Do not, *do not miss*, Harold Rosenberg and *The Walk*, opening next Saturday at—Café Heaven. Bring candles. You *do not* miss it," said the poet.

"Café Heaven. *You don't go there to eat, you go there to be fed.*"

Poets are often prophetic.

"You know, in the end it won't matter," said Harold.

"What?" said Shirley.

"All those degrees, certificates, awards, trophies, all the stuff on the bookshelves in my home office."

"And? . . ." Shirley knew. And they continued to stand in the middle of the coffeehouse. Surrounded.

"Well, I can think of another use for that office."

"What?" said Shirley.

"I want to adopt."

"A child?"

"No . . . children," said Harold.

"Children?"

And Shirley and Harold Rosenberg looked at each other.

She nodded.
And then they went back

to hugging.

"Do you think we qualify?" whispered Shirley, buried in Harold's hug.
"We didn't . . . but now we do," said Harold.

And the foregoing, shortly thereafter, was written by Shirley Rosenberg
. . . in her Chronicle. Somewhat, word for word. Style and all. Hugs and all.

T+

29.

Feet to the Ground
for the Special Thing

June 15, Saturday morning 6:00 a.m.

Tempie Teagarden woke up.
But didn't open her eyes —
She held them. Shut.
And then slowly opened them.
There was a blankness to her stare.
A blankness that meant . . . *clean slate.*

She spun her little body around and rested her feet on the little platform of her bed.
She looked at the floor, one foot below the little platform.
She remembered the days when she would stop . . . and stay. Stay in bed. Not leave. Stay frozen.
Stop. Thought taken captive. Gone. Never again.
I'm looking forward. Next step, then the next. Then the next.
. . .

She looked at her feet.
"Are you up for this?"
Her toes wiggled.
"You sure?"
Her toes wiggled.

"Okay, then you lead the way."

Her feet floated to the ground and touched the bruised and polished concrete floor. She felt the earth radiate up her body.

She looked at the little sofa across from her bed. It was empty as she thought it would be.

And she went straight to her little writing desk. And she set her timer for fifty minutes.

And she wrote.

This is what she wrote:

Counseling session 100, with the Lord.

Lord! I made it. The Hundredfold Blessing. I made it. I'm here. And, I'm alive. Father God, it all comes down to this day. This is it. This is what I've been striving for, for the last year.

And, there's only one thing that got me through. My commitment to reach One Hundred counseling sessions with You.

And, I did it.

I'm here.

And I'm going to write down everything that comes on my heart, and whatever, whatever You . . . say to me.

So, talk to me. I'm here. I'm listening. I hear You as clear as ever, right here in my heart.

"Tempie, let the day unfold for you. Be at peace. My peace. You have been faithful, and I will honor that."

Lord, I know. I feel it in my heart. Faithfulness is such a gift. It's Your gift to us. To me. Thank You.

Thank You for my little feet. At times, all I could do is look at them in the morning and say, *hey, you lead the way, and I'll follow.*

It was best when they followed You.

That was just so sweet, I can't tell You.

I have the cutest little feet.

Anyway, where was I?

. . .

Lord, today's the day. I know what I'm thinking and I'm sorry. I just want to say I'm sorry. I know what's going on in the back of my head. That I'm testing You. Lord, everything has gone so right, and so wrong with my Café. I still don't have a permit to open it, there's still fire- life-safety issues, and I can't get approval. The city turned on the electricity again yesterday. Just to allow us to test the systems, the equipment, everything. Well, the Café is ready, but if the City doesn't let me open it, I'm lost. And Norm and everyone who invested so much in the Café, and me, will have lost everything. I'll be wiped out. I'm afraid that will crush my faith. I'm afraid I'll go back to my pills. Lord, I don't mean to test You. That's wrong. But You know all my thoughts.

There's something else I'm thinking. I'm thinking what Pastor Jonathan always says: That You created each of us to do a special thing. A "Special Thing." Pastor Jonathan says that this is a Special Thing picked out for each of us that You, Father God want to happen here on Earth. That You *need* to happen here on earth. Sure, I know, You can always get someone else to do it, but no one can do that Special Thing exactly like the one You picked to do it.

Lord, I just know . . . the Café . . . is my Special Thing. Well, I admit, I suppose I'll know by the end of the day . . . whether, this is my Special Thing.

Lord, will Jonathan be there today? . . .

Hmmm, I'm not hearing nothing from You on that one . . .

Lord, thank You for Nick. Lord, why, oh why, has he been there for me the whole way? He has served me, the Café, all of us. He's been so faithful. I don't deserve him. Why Lord, why has he done that? I don't understand? I'm not used to people wanting to help me. Caring about me. But, today's the day. All year, I just hoped and prayed he would stick with me for this year. I had no right whatsoever to expect that. But he did. He stuck with me. Wow!

Lord, but after today, I release him. I will tell myself—to release him. To let him go. I only told him I love him five times over the last six months. I held it down pretty well. I'm laughing. I would have told him five times a day if I could have. I love him so much . . . it just simply, has not faded. I sort of wished it did. But it didn't. Love.

Anyway, thank You so much for him. After today, I'll be okay. If he leaves, he leaves. I'll deal with it. I'll let go.

And with that, I have to admit, I'm hoping I have at least one customer today. I better. Mercy, Lord, the place is huge. Norm sank a fortune in the place. By the way, why did he do that? Is he crazy? And Becky, his wife. Wow! Could I ever be a woman like her, Lord? So simple so certain. She is *so certain of You*. Lord, that woman knows You. Yes, I know You much better now, thanks to all Your counseling over the last year, but she really seems to know You. Wow, her tablecloths. What's with them? You've really placed a blessing on them. It's just some kind of miracle. Anyway, thank You for Becky also.

Lord, what's this Hundredfold Blessing all about? Why did You want me to get this far? And where do I go from here?

"Tempie, I have a plan for you, and that plan is being revealed. Your faith is strong. The path is lit. You shall be a blessing to many. Stay the course."

Lord, I'm sorry, but I still can't help but ask You, I'll be breaking a bunch of laws today. I'm opening my Café, without a permit. And the power could be cut at anytime. Well, it's guaranteed to be cut at 9:00 p.m. tonight no matter what—that's what the last NOTICE said. It was only long enough to test systems.

Lord, mercy. I'm breaking laws aren't I? What do I do?

"Dear Tempie, be patient, have faith. Open your Café this morning. At 8:00 a.m."

But Lord, what about all those laws?

"You're not breaking any laws. The coffeehouse, the building, everything is in perfect condition. The City just doesn't know that yet."

But it's Saturday, no inspector will come on a Saturday—other than to shut us down!

"Tempie . . ."

Lord, You didn't finish Your thought. Now You have me worried. I'm not supposed to worry.

"Tempie, it's time to get ready. I want you there at 8:00 a.m. sharp."

Okay, Lord.

It's okay, *I'll follow my little feet.*

I'm sorry for doing all the talking.

Lord, will anyone show up?

"Tempie! It's time."

Okay, okay, I'm getting ready.

End of counseling session 100, with the Lord.

Tempie took some time to take a shower, clean her little studio apartment, dress, and head to her car.

She tried to fight off her anxiousness. The Café is to open at 8:00 a.m. sharp, and her group insisted she get a good night's sleep. They would take care of everything. They would get there early with all the staff, they would have everything set to go right on time.

And it was time for her, to just get rest and be there.

At 8:00 a.m. The culmination of one year of planning, dreaming, and work.

Tempie headed for her car.

She hopped in her car and started driving. She felt she was in slow motion. The car seemed to drive itself. Down the hills.

It was 7:45 a.m. when she took a left on Sunset Boulevard, heading toward the Echo Park area. She knew this drive so well. She had done it hundreds of times over the last year, ever since Nick found this huge abandoned warehouse in a rundown area of Sunset.

It was 7:50 a.m. She was driving south on Sunset. And the traffic started backing up. And she lost it. She had to stop, and now she was further blocking traffic. She just started crying so hard, she couldn't take it.

Where did the tears come from? She had poured everything
. . . everything . . .

Then the traffic started to creep forward just a little. Her
eyes were plastered on the car in front of her. She was within
blocks . . .

And she noticed. There were people on the sidewalk.
Lined up . . . for what?
She saw the line on the left. Running along the sidewalk.
And then she knew.
The line started blocks before the Café. It couldn't be the
Café?
And she saw Nick. He was serving coffee.
To the people in line.
He actually had a cart. And she saw the cups. Pope Francis
Coffee. There were friends from the Outreach Center; they were
also serving people in line.
They were serving the people in line.

And it was a line. To get into the coffeehouse. And the traffic
wasn't going anywhere.
And then she saw Norm, Harold, Baby Doe 1, and Bentley
approach her car.
They invited her out of her car, as Bentley jumped in to
take over and park it.

And they led her five blocks to the entrance of Café Heaven.
And she was still crying.

And then Nick was there.
And that was it.
She fainted.
  But he caught her.

It was 8:00 a.m.

T+

30.

Café Heaven

I decided that I had to be really honest with you. So much had happened in a year that we had become some sort of one. One what I don't know. I was so caught up in it, that I didn't know what it was, and I didn't care. I was so into it, that my life
. . .

Anyway, I asked everyone, Tempie, Nick, Harold, and Baby Doe 1 to put it in their own words. So much came together that day.

The day we opened Café Heaven.

I had worked twenty-four hours straight. My wife Becky was right beside me, and literally an army of helpers. You can't imagine. You know, the bottom line is . . . that Café Heaven is big. Really big. Nick truly was insane. And, if we indeed did open on the morning of June 15th, at 8:00 a.m., we would be breaking a mountain of laws. We had no permit. None. No final inspection.

But this was the date we kept hearing.

This was the day.

It was 5:00 a.m., when someone came to the door at Café Heaven. It's a narrow door, for such a large place.

But, it is narrow.

She walked up, and I was the first to see her.

She said, "Is Café Heaven open yet?"

And that was it. The first time I heard the name "Café Heaven" from someone I didn't know.

My first thought was, *do we even have the sign up yet?* We didn't. But, Nick quickly grabbed a small table and let her sit outside on the sidewalk, and . . . he got her a cup of Pope Francis coffee. In case anyone wants to know someday, that was the first ever cup of Pope Francis coffee served.

We never took further notice of the woman until much later in the day. She stayed put. And that was okay with us.

But, that was at 5:00 a.m. And by 6:00 a.m., fifteen more tables were out on the sidewalk, and by 6:30 a.m. we had run out of tables. Someone came to the rescue, and by 7:00 a.m. tables filled with people extended three blocks out — both directions. The abandoned neighborhood didn't seem so abandoned anymore. Turns out Nick had planned for this. He surprised us with coffee carts, handcrafted of course at . . . the Outreach Center. And there he was serving . . . coffee and peace muffins.

The bottom line is that by 8:00 a.m. we had filled out five blocks in both directions. We had no permit to use the sidewalk.

And that didn't include the line that had also formed . . .

because . . . still, no customer had yet . . . entered the Café, through that narrow door.

I was wondering if we would all be in jail by midnight.

Yep, Nick had a lot of foresight. We were close to the Outreach Center. We had an endless supply of helpers. And by 8:00 a.m. it was no longer clear who was a host, a server, a busboy, a customer, a friend, a tourist, a beggar, or a thief. What was clear was that . . .

no one left . . .

and I was already seeing something, that made me smile . . . with a small breeze they flapped just a little bit.

Becky's tablecloths.

The only time I looked up in those last rushed hours before the opening was at 7:50 a.m. I got word that Tempie was approaching in her car. The traffic was jammed. We had to get her. 8:00 a.m. was approaching.

And we were going to open.
No matter what.

And we did.
And I asked everyone, to put it in their own words.
. . .

My name is Tempie Teagarden. Norm told each of us that
it was time for him to complete the last chapter of this book, *The
Problem Solver*, and that each of us would be contributing. He
asked me to go first, told me to keep it short and just highlight a
few things from that first-day opening of Café Heaven.
So, here goes.

June 15, Saturday morning, 7:58 a.m.

I'm Chinese. *Yes,* sorry if I burst your bubble and you
pictured something different. But I wanted to get that out
right away in case you were wondering. I'm thirty years old,
and before this last year of *Anno Domini,* I felt old. It was the
depression, my *everyday suit.*
When I emerged from my car driving down Sunset
Boulevard, I heard church bells. The most beautiful church bells,
and I looked around and saw people everywhere, and this long
line going down the sidewalk, and I didn't want to believe, but
I knew, they were people lined up to go to Café Heaven. And I
just started crying because everything in my life came together
in that one moment. I don't want to bore you with the details
of my life, but my family immigrated here to the United States
when I was two, and they were determined to be westernized,
especially my mom. Very disciplined, we lived this high-end
life in New York, and all my brothers and sisters were educated
at the best colleges in the country, and all live substantial
professional lives, have all the goodies, and families, big houses,
and expensive cars—except me.
I was the failure in the family.

It turns out that my family came from a long history of
Teagardens (my mom's *loose,* Americanized translation of my

Chinese name) who ran tea and coffeehouses in China. Tea and coffee is in our blood. And what I learned from my counseling sessions with the Lord, although it took about twenty-five sessions before it sank in—is that God had always had a Plan for me to open a coffeehouse in the United States, and He told me what to do. Finally, I got out of the way.

So, let's just say that, I didn't just open a little coffeehouse in the Echo Park area of Los Angeles. *Apparently*, the Lord had this Plan for me, shall we say, for a long time. Oh, and . . . the cafe—it isn't little.

And in that one moment:

7:58 a.m. *I knew.*

Have you ever had that feeling?

I knew.

If you haven't, please, please, please, seek it out.

And the church bells rang, I looked up, and I saw the sign. And it was the Problem Solver, up on a ladder, and he seemed to be making the last adjustments.

Café Heaven.

Of course, this was nothing I could have done on my own. But I don't need to tell you that.

I knew from my counseling sessions that there was something even bigger that could happen later in the day.

And, it was to happen. Later.

So, I just started crying. Why not get started early?

And, at 8:00 a.m., the exact time, on the exact day, the Lord told me to open Café Heaven, I saw . . . *that it would open!*

And I fainted.

Into the arms of someone I was so in love with I couldn't stand it.

. . .

My name is Nick Tate. I'm thirty-one years old. And I gave it everything I could. To be an actor. But, let's be honest. It never felt right.

It was a judge who ordered me to go see the Problem Solver, or, I was going to jail—right then and there. Straight to jail, or straight to see the Problem Solver. I was in a courtroom on the fifth floor, and I was ordered to the ninth floor. It was so weird. I was thinking as I left the courtroom that, *the judge didn't even tell me to report back. There was no return date. Weird.*

Then I thought, well, what the heck, I'll go see this Problem Solver. He wouldn't be hard to fool. I could buy some time, and then, back to my acting gigs or ... *trying to get* my acting gigs. In the past, I had only gone back to drugs.

Talk about strange when I got to the ninth floor cafeteria. There were two lines. I just got in the right line. Whatever. Just get in line. You got to get in line to see this guy. This Problem Solver.

Yes, I spoke with an Intern. And yes, I patiently waited in line. Kind of moving up, chair by chair.

And then I was sitting in front of him.

And he looked at me.

And he said: "Are you ready?"

— *This* was someone I couldn't fool. That's it. My barriers fell. I'm sorry, I don't get this, but they did. They just fell off.

And he was still looking at me, and he said: "Do you want to do this on your own strength or on God's strength?"

I knew, I had to answer this question one way only. There was no other way.

And I looked at this person I had never seen before and I said:

"I want to do this on God's strength."

And he was still looking at me. But he wasn't really looking at me. He was looking *with* me. He was *excited* about things I didn't even see. He said:

"I know you do. Let's get started."

And we did.

It was only fifteen minutes later that I went back to that courtroom on the fifth floor, and I interrupted a hearing. And I asked the judge if it would be okay if I approached the bench to hug him.

Some of us had to wait longer than others to find a group. But eventually . . . well you should know by now, it just happened.

And then *Anno Domini* happened and suddenly I had a plan for one year. A Plan. But I really didn't know it was my plan.

What you don't know is that . . . when Tempie almost took her life at the six-month mark, I started spending the night at her little apartment sleeping on a sofa across from her bed. The group was simply not not not going to risk her doing something stupid again. So that's what I did. I slept on that sofa for six months night after night. And I never touched her.

It was weird at first. I kind of felt like a guard or something. At times I felt like an angel. I was never going to allow anything, *anything*, to happen to this girl. I'm six-foot-two, 225 pounds. And, if I must say — solid.

I heard every little peep out of that girl for six months.

And something happened somewhere along the way. I felt like she was guarding me. All my fears went away. Fears of relapse, fears of loneliness, fears of a lifetime. I wasn't going to do anything, *anything to me*, that would hurt this girl. I was on assignment.

We weren't sleeping together before marriage, we were guarding together.

So . . . this is what happened. I might as well tell you.

And it happened on that first day . . .

the first day of

Café Heaven.

Nope, I can't do it. I'll crack up. And I'm too tough for that. Norm's gotta do this one for me.

I ain't no writer anyway.

I keep a Chronicle. That I'm good at. But I have a Friend to help me. Seems I need a friend for everything.

You'll hear from Norm on this one.

. . .

But Norm's not up yet. I'm up next.

My name is Harold Rosenberg. I'm a lawyer.

Mediocrity brought me to the table. To the group. That's why I went to the ninth floor. That's why anyone suffering from my condition needs to seek out the Problem Solver. My condition is rampant. The lukewarms.

I'm proud of myself. Can I take a moment? I hit the big 100. One Hundred counseling sessions with the Lord. I did it the night before . . .
that first day at Café Heaven.
Now it all seems so obvious. But way too obvious for a smart guy like me to see.

I'm a lawyer. I was never short on words. I was short on everything else. I'm already into my second Chronicle. I asked Norm if I could write this whole last chapter. I figured there'd be an award for it, another certificate for the shelves. Isn't it nice? No more awards, I chased them my whole life. Now, Shirley and I are just going to box them up.
Finally,
because something else had fired me up over that last year . . . and that led to a meeting that was to take place
. . . on that first day at Café Heaven.
And it happened in the morning.

I was so torn that morning. I was a nervous wreck. Because of the meeting, *and*, because my harp was going to be returned to me. Shirley had taken it the night after I had pushed it over. I figured I had destroyed it. I never saw it again, well, until that first morning. It was to come back to me,
At 10:00 a.m.
But, Shirley and I also had the meeting to attend to. Because of schedules it had to be at 10:00 a.m. The same time.
The Café was full by then. But a table was reserved for us. Shirley and me. And the adoption agency. They were pinpoint on time. Two of them. All the questions were easy, and I felt nothing would ever be in my hands again. I was slowly letting go of everything . . . *every thing*, I thought I had control over . . .
and it all just lifted away.

The only question that mattered was something like: "What kind of child do you want to adopt?"

Shirley said, "the next one abandoned and left at the Outreach Center. We want to be on the list, for the next one."

And I added, "and the next one."

"How many?" the person asked.

And I said: "We'll let you know when to stop."

It wasn't too long of a meeting. I have to tell you, as the meeting ended, the buzz of the energy in a packed Café started to come up, like the volume of a new life . . . so I decided to look up from the table,

. . . and there it was,

my harp.

It had returned.

And there was this arc of people behind it. And I recognized them all. The craftsmen. And I saw the sparrow logo on my harp. So little so certain. And the number, No. 00101. Guard your heart, guard your harp.

I was never again . . . going to let either of them down.

So, possibly you can see why I asked Norm if I could write this whole chapter, because of just the things that happened to me . . . in just one day.

So, one other thing.

Look, I don't want to jump ahead or anything, but Norm will fill in the gaps later. That's our Norm.

But, the lights were going to go out. At 9:00 p.m. The City was going to turn the electricity off, throw us out — and there were a lot of us, and shut the place down at 9:00 p.m. And I tried for six months to make sure we'd get the permit. I'm a lawyer, I should be good for something. But all my efforts had failed. But, in a counseling session one week before the opening, I was told what to do.

And this is what happened:

Well, at 9:00 p.m. just about the time a certain little ceremony was starting up at the Café, the lights indeed were cut off. Out. Period. They shut us down. And I waited and I prayed.

And, remember that lady, the first one to arrive at 5:00 a.m.? Well, suddenly she was in the Café. As if right on cue. And she held up a candle for this certain little ceremony that had started. And she lit it. And then I saw my poet friend from the coffeehouse. Remember her, playing the guitar? And she lit a candle. And suddenly everyone had a candle. And hundreds of candles were lit. And you know

those candles lit up the Café, and then out the door, and up the sidewalks for as far as one could see,

and the whole neighborhood

and they made the headlines the next morning: *Café Heaven Lights up Echo Park.*

And just about the time I knew we'd all be arrested, the City showed up. A whole group of them. And they told us we'd have to leave — and to put out the candles.

And, there was dead silence.

And there was this breeze . . .

. . . well, you remember that elderly couple, badges and clipboard, who always just seemed to hang around. Norm and I would notice them at the courthouse, at the cafeteria, at the Outreach Center. Well, he works for the City. He's the senior inspector. And there he was. With his wife, always beside him — and with the clipboard. In a counseling session I was told to track him down and ask him to come. And please help us. Nothing I had done had helped.

He was the grouchiest old curmudgeon I could imagine. He didn't know how to smile.

But when I asked him to come, one week before the Café was to open — *illegally* that is, he looked at me and said:

"You gonna play that harp?"

I said, "Yes."

"Then I'll be there. And that place better be perfect or I'll shut it down. Ain't nobody going to not be safe in my territory."

And there he was. A little late. But on time.

And the candles stayed lit.

And everyone stayed in place.

And the little ceremony took place.

And we waited.

. . .

And I get to tell you about the ceremony. Because I was the photographer. Yours truly, *Baby Doe 1*. I'm a photographer. Has anyone told you that yet?

Well, here's how it came down:

At about 8:45 p.m., just about sundown on the warm, summery night in Los Angeles, Nick went looking for Tempie and found her in the middle of the Café.

And he stopped her in her tracks.

And, everyone was there. Everyone. I mean the place was packed. And Harold was playing his harp with his band of rejects, *The Walk*. I don't know what he was playing. He doesn't even know. But it was perfect.

And Nick, always short on words, simply looked at Tempie and said:

"Tempie Teagarden, I'm in love with you. You are truly the most incredible, the most beautiful woman I've ever met. Will you marry me?"

Well, she was scared or something and she said, "No."

"No?" said Nick. And I clicked away anyway. But I had no breath.

. . .

There was this long pause.

"What I mean by 'no' is 'yes,'" said Tempie. And the place was so quiet. *The Walk* was down to one note at a time.

"Well, I need a better 'yes' than 'no,'" said Nick.

And Tempie looked up. And it was a long look. And she said:

"Yes." And then she launched. She somehow took several steps back and then ran and jumped into Nick's arms. Picture a beanstalk jumping into the arms of an oak tree. You get the picture—but I took it.

It's now on the wall of the gallery.

The gallery at the back of Café Heaven where I had my first showing. The day that Café Heaven opened. The theme:

Forgiveness. And all in black and white. With one exception. Just one color photograph. And, it wasn't even a photo I took because something else happened to me that day.

Indeed, it had already happened.

At 3:00 p.m. Just after my show had technically opened at 2:00 p.m. in the gallery at the Café.

Norm came to get me. There was someone to see me. A person named "Gwen." So I went to the front of the Café, and a woman was seated at the counter. And I sat next to her.

The woman looks at me.

"I was hoping you were still alive."

I saw tears. There were deep valleys they flowed down through.

"You can never forgive me for what I did to you. Never.

"I wanted to know . . . you lived.

"But — I just can't believe I found you."

I looked at her. The woman is about forty-five. Same color hair. Same face. Same nose . . . *as me*. I felt a little scared. "Who are you?"

"Just a little nothin'" . . . and she sobbed as she looked away.

And then Bentley walked up.

And I knew.

I stood up. I had to.

The woman slowly stood up. And started to leave.

And I watched her walk away. She left the Café.

. . . And then I ran after her . . .

And Bentley picked up my camera.

And took a picture.

. . . of a mother and daughter. Hugging.

The only color photo.

. . .

Well, I don't know about you, but I'm just about done here. Norm Adams at your service. Let me tell you just a few more things and then
I'm done.

Well, for starters, *the ceremony*. Baby Doe 1 left you hanging. After Tempie said "Yes!" well, Nick looked at her, there in his arms that is, and we heard him say quietly, "Now."
Tempie said, "Now? Right now? Right here." And Nick slowly let her down to the ground, which for Tempie was always a long ways off.
The place was silent. One note at a time.
"Yes. Now."
And Tempie looked around, and saw all the faces. Mercy, hundreds of faces. People packed in like you can't imagine.
"Everybody I've ever really known is here. I'm so glad I started early this morning. To cry, that is. . . . Don't we need a—"
And then he walked up. Pastor Jonathan from the Outreach Center.
And then Tempie really lost it.
What a smile he had.
Jonathan looked at us all and said, "I'm not supportive of one-minute engagements. But I'm very supportive of guarding together before marriage. And that's what happened here. So, I'm ready, if they are."
They both nodded.
We *all* nodded.
We were all somehow completing something.
Remember, we still didn't have electricity. No lights. But amazing *light*. Candles by the hundreds. Out the Café and up the streets, but Harold told you that. The side streets had been blocked off by now by the police. And we waited. The Café, everything, was in the hands of the inspector, and his wife with the clipboard. Old school.
And he walked the whole place as the ceremony began.
The Problem Solver was there . . . and he stood up for Tempie. I stood up for Nick.

Look, I can't do this part. The ceremony, the music. Turns out Harold recorded the whole night. It's a big seller at the Café. Listen to the music. Which really means listen to the music . . . in your heart.

Oh, and guess who's our cook? Tikipas! Yep. He lost his farm to bankruptcy. Now that would have surely tested my faith, but not his. Nope. Not him. He just got a new calling. Turns out he had always been a totally fantastic cook. And it was he who put together the kitchen, all the cooks, and made all the arrangements for the food at the Café. He knew everything. He knew what to do. Oh, and don't gripe at me about this next point, but after raising all those cows and all, somehow he arranged in the bankruptcy to save the ones that remained, and they were freed up. Apparently, the land was worth more than the cows, I don't know. But Tikipas became a vegetarian. I know, I know, some of my friends are going to slam me for this one. Heck, I used to live at steakhouses.

Anyway, don't worry, the Café is not vegetarian, but if you give Tikipas a chance he'll change everything about the way you eat. I'm a new man, slim, trim, and . . . in love. Becky's sitting next to me as I write this. I was on the road to open-heart surgery, chest pains every day, overweight, and an early death.

Yes, yes. It was at about 11:00 p.m. that the elderly couple, i.e. the inspector and his wife were done. But come on? That guy never smiled. But . . . turns out, he liked to play the guitar. And during the last part of the inspection, he sat in with *The Walk*. I'd love to know what they played. It's on the record.

And we got our "A" in the window of the Café.

And let's just say, I finally got a read on what those badges said.

My ribs are getting sore. Becky keeps hitting me. Okay, yes, a whole slew of my friends from work showed up at the Café. And yes, the Board had voted to make me president of the company and I said I'd do it, if they let me take on a new assignment, if and when it comes. And they just said "yes." But at least one Board member asked: "What new assignment?"

All I could say was, "I don't know, and I don't know when."

And that was it.

And at the end of the day, I felt I just had one more thing to do at the Café. Go talk to Tikipas. And apologize.

So, I go looking for Tikipas and I find him in, where else, but the kitchen and I corner him. And I muster up a little strength. And this is what happened:

"Look, I need to apologize for something. It goes way back to when I first saw you at the courthouse, in the elevator, and in the cafeteria. I need to —"

But, Tikipas says: "No, let me go first." And he's kind of big, so I let him.

Tikipas looks down at me with his big brown eyes and says:

"You know, when I first saw you, I thought you looked like the most stiff-necked, uptight, stuck-up, out-of-shape bore on the planet . . . etc., etc. So, I want to apologize. For my thoughts." He gave me this kind of sheepish look.

And I just stood there.

And then he said, "What do you want to apologize for?"

And I started to chuckle. And then I started laughing. And then, I think he knew, and he started laughing.

And now we both lose it in laughter.

And the servers, busboys, and helpers notice, and they start laughing.

And then the customers.

And everyone is laughing.

. . .

I guess it's called holy laughter.
And it went on for five or ten minutes.
And the Café became known for such outbursts, and the narrow door, and the size of the place, and the little tables, and the tablecloths, and the mugs, and the photography,
and the music, the peace muffins with the little messages,
and the coffee of course,
and a lot of other things.

And, the people.
. . .

The End.

Epilogues
and
Letters

Epilogue 1

Anno Domini Two

Sunday morning. June 16. 3:00 a.m.

Café Heaven is still open.

And, it's buzzing with customers, servers, cooks, staff, guests, friends, everyone.

Norm Adams goes looking for his friends. He thinks he'll find them toward the back. Near the photography gallery.

And there they were.

Tempie leaned against Nick, who leaned against Baby Doe 1, who leaned against Harold. Bentley and Tikipas crashed into each other. All on the same sofa. The Café is big; so are the sofas.

Norm sat in a chair across from them. And looked them over.

"Guys, don't wake up, but I just want to talk to you.

"The year is over.

"*Anno Domini* One, has come to an end . . .

"I know what we're supposed to do, and I'm here to tell you.

"But first, I want to thank each of you. I've been so blessed to know you, to work with you, to just be with you. So I want to thank you.

"... and, of course apologize for the times I left us hanging, unprotected, just out there. I won't let it happen again, I promise. You can count on me ...

"Anyway,
"we're supposed to do it again,
"*Anno Domini* Two.
"I think it's good to catch up to your dreams. And I really have with all of you. With my wife and kids. So many great things have happened to me this year.
"But, I know that I know that I know,
"we're supposed to do it again.
"*Anno Domini* Two.
"Make new dreams. Build on old dreams. Stay on track."

Becky walks up, with a tray of coffees.
And the group starts to shake themselves awake.

"Don't worry, it's decaf."
"Sacrilegious," said Nick and he opens his eyes.
"Well, maybe put that in the letter to Pope Francis when we ask if we can use his name on our coffee: *Is decaf coffee sacrilegious?* It probably is, but you, Nick Tate, have a honeymoon to get to, and the rest of us, well, we're just taste testing.
"Anyway, the bottom line is, we had a pretty good year.
"So, I say, let's do it again. *Anno Domini* Two.
"Agreed?"
"Yes," they all say one by one as they open their eyes, including Bentley and Tikipas.
. . .

"Good, let's meet next Saturday, 3:00 p.m. at the Outreach Center. Same place, the War Room. *Anno Domini* Two."
"If you catch up to your dreams,
". . . time to make new ones."

Tempie was still shaking herself awake. "You know . . ." She hesitated.
Norm looked at her. "Spit it out, Tempie."

"Well, I was wondering if we can do *Anno Domini* the rest of our lives, year by year . . . together."

And they all looked up.
Then slowly . . . stood up.
Each one of them.

And they lifted their cups . . .

of Pope Francis coffee.

Epilogue 2

Is It Time?

Time slipped by, and one day we received word that the Problem Solver passed away.

The funeral at Angelus Temple was huge, and so was the wake at Café Heaven. Same story, the police had to block off the side streets around the Café. And on that day, we served thirty thousand people. At *least* thirty thousand. Which, by the way, wasn't all that hard. The Outreach Center feeds thirty thousand people each week. They just had to step it up. Which is what they always do.

Before the funeral and after, everyone was looking at me.
I knew why, I have to admit.
I know, I know, I already felt it in my heart.
But, who am I? Why me?
And then I received a letter from the courthouse.
So, on a Monday morning, I went down to the courthouse.

And, this is what happened:

I arrived at 8:00 a.m.
I got in line. I went through security. And I got in the elevator. As I was riding up, there was a woman who looked at me and I knew where she was going.

So I asked her:

"Have you decided?"

She looked at me, and frankly, I was really surprised. Why, oh why, did her tears start to flow?

"Yes, I have. I decided to do it on the Lord's strength. It's simple, I can't do this on my own."

I looked at her.

"I know what you mean." And I never knew so much joy in my heart. She and I, and many others rode up the elevator.

When I got off, there was a huge group, mostly security officers, court staff members, lots of citizens, and of course, you know who:

The Young Woman with the skier's cap.
The Actor with long hair and tattoos.
The Professional Man, in a business suit.
And, the Everyday Woman, in her everyday suit.

For us, everything had changed, but for me, the way I first saw Baby Doe 1, Nick, Harold and Tempie . . . is, still, so special to me.

I was led to the set of tables in the middle of the cafeteria. And there were twelve Chronicles laid out on the center table:

1st Chronicle
The life and future of Daniel.

Through,

12th Chronicle
The life and future of Daniel.

And next to the Chronicles was the pen. His pen.

"TPS left them here for you," said a security officer. "And here's his note."

I read the note. But I have to tell you. I'm not going to share it with you just now. But soon. Well, except for one thing. He asked me to ask each of you, if, perhaps it's time? Time for you to have your first counseling session with *the* Counselor?

And I picked up the pen. I felt its weight. How many people had used this pen to place their name on the cover of their 1st Chronicle? And how many to come?
Don't let your story go unwritten.

Well, I can tell you the joy I felt was immense.

I looked at everyone.
I looked at two long lines.
And I said:
"Let's get to work."

Tikipas jumped in front of me:
"Intern One at your service."
And I nodded.
Nick Tate jumped in front of me:
"Intern Two at your service."
And I nodded.
Tempie Teagarden jumped in front of me:
"Intern Three at your service."
And I nodded.

And then, Baby Doe 1, Harold, Bentley, and too many others to count, were there.

. . . And, the most incredible and beautiful woman in the world, my wife,
Becky, was there. And, yes, she had already set one of her tablecloths on the counseling table. *I wouldn't want to be without that.*

Oh, and one other thing:
One of the security guards walked up to me with an old herringbone jacket which, of course, we all recognized.

And . . . I tried it on. And it fit.

I couldn't help but notice his name sewn inside the coat, left side. "Daniel." And under his name he had sewn, "Norm Adams." And, yes, I noticed the

T+

sewn in above his name just a little to the left.
Trust the Lord.

And, with the help of more people than I can tell you, I sat down.

And, I went to work.

Amen.

Letter to Pope Francis

You Only Pope Once

His Holiness, Pope Francis
Apostolic Palace
00120 Vatican City

Dear Pope Francis,

Look, here's the thing. I know you're busy, what with all the prayers and everything that needs to go around. But, I wanted to propose a simple way of saving the world, *in a practical sense*, that is.

Anyway:

You need to update the blessing for coffee. Look, here's the deal, we all know about how Pope Clement VIII blessed coffee in 1600 and all. That was cool, but—you need to take it to a new level. And we know you're a coffee lover! You've been spotted drinking Ristretto in coffeehouses in Rome. Ristretto, bolder, fuller, with more body and less bitterness. Now that's the kind of Pope we've needed. So, we figured you would do it.

I just opened a new coffeehouse in the Los Angeles area. Yes, *the City of Angels*. It's called Café Heaven. I got permission from the Big Guy on that one. But, we named our coffee *Pope Francis coffee.*

Well, I feel it necessary to get your permission, even though we already started doing it. You see . . . well, God saved me. Yep.

From horrible never-ending depression, an attempted suicide, and a bunch of other things. Now, I'm leading the abundant life, and, well, this really is happiness. I believe I'm right in the middle of the *Special Thing* that God created me for. So, I'm trying to do everything right. Will you give us your permission to use your name on our coffee? I know it's a lot to ask, but we're all really good people who are so blessed, I can't tell you, and all we want to do is be a blessing to others.

And, well, miracles are coming from your coffee. I can't explain it, but they are. There's something special about the taste. Look, I use *Caffea Arabica* beans and we do a really good job of brewing the coffee, but something special is going on. People come from everywhere to drink Pope Francis coffee. And they sip the coffee on tables with Becky Adams' tablecloths, and then there's a double blessing. Well, I can't handle it all, but I know I was called to send you this letter to get your permission to continue to use your name on our coffee, but . . . much more important, to get you to bless *all* coffee.

All coffee! Could you do that?

Well, here at my coffeehouse, we have every kind of people imaginable. All kinds. It looks like heaven here. All colors, all sizes, all ages, all countries, all religions, all political persuasions, all differences imaginable . . . but, something's special here. This place is blessed. There's so much peace. And, we all drink coffee. Yes, there's some tea drinkers and all, but it's the coffee that's doing it. If coffee were blessed, blessed around the world, think of it. All cups of coffee will be touched by the hand of God, and I just know that God wants us to live at peace with each other. He wants us to love each other.

I have to tell you something. I'm so in love with my husband, Nick, and he says hello. But, it gets better. I'm pregnant!!! Wow!!! How could I be more happy? Heck (sorry), it probably happened the first night after we got married. — I should have gotten pregnant the first time I looked at him, but it doesn't work that way. He's so big and strong, that, well,

anyway, where was I?

Oh, the blessing. You see, it's so hard to see me and Nick bringing in a child to this world. But, if you blessed all the coffee in the world, then my baby will find a more peaceful world when she (I'm convinced she's a girl) grows up, and I want that more than anything. For my baby, and everyone.

Here's my suggestion for a blessing, but feel free to use your own:

Dear God,

In the name of Jesus, I hereby bless all coffee, anywhere in the world. All cups brewed and drank today, and all future cups brewed and drank, right here, and for all time, and for all people.

I bless it in the name of Jesus that each cup be infused with the Holy Spirit, causing the person who drinks it to be a person of peace first, then love. A person of compassion, a seeker of reconciliation, a seeker of understanding, a seeker of acceptance, and lastly, a seeker of You, Heavenly Father.

In Jesus' name I pray.

Amen.

How's that? Simple, right? Please consider having a counseling session with the Lord, and see what He says. He put me up to this.

Anyway, that's my pitch. I did the best I could.

Please let us know when you get the job done. We're already believing—it is done!

From the great unwashed masses, but blessed nonetheless, we send you our love and prayers from the City of Angels.

Where the angels — are out in force.

Thank you so much.

Tempie Teagarden
Café Heaven
Los Angeles, California
USA

Letter to Harold Rosenberg

The Wounded Instrument

Dear Harold,

Your wife, Shirley contacted me in December of last year. It was good to hear from you through your wife after such a long time. Yes, I'm still alive. Even I can't believe it. But apparently it is for a reason, because to hear that your harp, No. 00101 had been damaged grieved me deeply. And to hear that you had gone back to playing it warmed my heart. I can still hear the notes from when you first played No. 00101, and I know the song isn't over.

I remember you well, Harold, although it has been indeed, thirty-five years since you picked up No. 00101. You were a young boy of twelve at the time and I remember that you were very intelligent. I felt sorry for you; I knew you would have to contend with that someday. And, I knew you would have to let it go. Congratulations, you have done that. You had wanted to play the great concert halls of the world; I'm so pleased to hear the type of concert halls you've found. First dreams are always the most authentic, found dreams the most satisfying.

I have enjoyed staying in contact with your wife over the past six months as we worked on the repair of your damaged No. 00101. She said you had intentionally pushed over the instrument. Certainly, it is rare that an instrument like this is pushed over. Of course I wondered what it was that you really pushed over. I trust that as I worked on the repair of your harp from afar, that the repair work on you has also progressed. And I should note that the technicians at the Outreach Center are outstanding in following directions. Their talents are noteworthy. No doubt they are highly schooled in the trade, and beyond that, gifted in the repair of the soul of a beloved instrument.

My friend, please know that a wounded instrument plays better than the original. You will find that it is more sympathetic, more attentive, more patient, and it will listen. But never again let sadness permeate it by neglect.

My life has been worth living if I can know in my heart that you will play your harp, No. 00101, the rest of your life. I'm eighty-nine now. I don't know how much time I have left. But, I send my love to you, my son, and know that when you see your repaired harp again at the opening of Café Heaven, and then play it again for the first time, you will know that,

all is healed.

Your old friend,

Hans Grundershun
Salzburg, Austria

Note to Baby Doe 1

A Little Nothin'

Dear Baby Doe 1,

I asked Tempie for a job today. I suppose word will get back to you, so I wanted to leave you this note. I'm way past anyone ever willing to give me a chance, but I asked Bentley and he told me to do it. He knows I just want to be close to you. No one will ever forgive me for what I did, for all the things I did. It was only Bentley who would try to look in on me on occasion over these last twenty-eight years. He never stopped trying to pull me around. But lately, seeing you from afar, watching you wait on tables, work at the restaurant, see you smile, and take your pictures, I sensed that I should try. Just ask. I have no faith in myself. But with a little help from Bentley, I asked Tempie if she'd let me do something around the Café, anything.

She looked at me. She said, "I recognize you." I told her "I'm just a little nothin'."

And she said, "I'm just a little nothin' myself. Sounds like you'll fit in."

Then she told me I could start by keeping the photography gallery clean and neat, and all the tables, chairs, and stuff in that area. She told me there was a meeting tomorrow. Quarterly checkup. *Anno Domini*. I was invited. Explanation to follow.

Other than Bentley, she's the only person who gave me a little hope.

I'm sitting across the street on the bench. I just need you to nod your head, and tell me this is okay with you. Or, if not.

Gwen

"I love talking to God. He seems to know everything."

Baby Doe 1

For the waywardness of the simple
will kill them,
and the complacency of fools
will destroy them.

Proverbs 1:32 (NIV)

Your very lives are a letter
   that anyone can read by just looking at you.
   Christ himself wrote it — not with ink,
   but with God's living Spirit;
   not chiseled into stone,
   but carved into human lives — and we publish it.

2 Corinthians 3:3 (The Message)

Acknowledgments

As I write this, I'm on a train from Madrid, Spain, to St. Jean Pied-de-Port in the south of France. It's an important birthday in my life and tomorrow, with perfect timing, I will start *The Way*. I will trek about 500 miles from the south of France to the western coast of Spain on The Way of St. James, and all I can think about is all the wonderful people I've had, and still have, in my life. I'm so thankful.

This book, *The Problem Solver*, felt downloaded from God from 3:00 a.m. until about 8:00 a.m. most days over a period of time fraught with tough court battles, stressful mediations, arbitrations, and a few nervous breakdowns. I hope in my heart, after thirty-five years of being at the crossroads of human conflict, and after so much in-depth counseling of so many people, that perhaps some of those that really, really want to solve their problems will read this book and remember that, ultimately, there is only one true source for problem solving.

I'd like to thank my friends and family who helped me so much through this process, as they did with my first book, *Settle It! . . . and be Blessed.* Here are some of them:

I'd like to thank my friends Phyllis Lombardi and Maryjo McCarley that I've known over the years at the Dream Center. They are always there for me and helped so much with this book, and with *Settle It! . . . and be Blessed.* Indeed, I'd like to thank all my friends at the Dream Center Los Angeles. I have so many friends there, and they all have played an amazing part in my life. Special thanks to Mona Lusk, Danny Ovando, Ida Somero, Kaci Davis, Mike Conner, Robert Sayles, Kelli Bradley, Jonathan Martinez, Todd Leader, Joel Bodker, Danny Slavens, and . . . Calvin.

And thank you Pastors Tommy and Matthew Barnett for too many reasons to list. It's Tommy's writing that inspired me to understand that God truly does have a "special thing" for each of us to do. Read Tommy's book, *The Power of the Half Hour*. Please read chapter three about that "special thing" that God created each of us to do. Read all of Matthew's books, especially *The Cause Within You* and *Misfits Welcome*, and you will understand why he and the Dream Center are such an inspiration to so many people, including me.

My mom, Jerry, is still working at eighty-five years old. Indeed, as a Certified Nurse Assistant, she took up residence at the Dream Center (the inspiration for the "Outreach Center" in this book) where she serves in their mobile medical clinic. What an amazing person and inspiration for me. God does make perfect moms and you are one of them. You inspire me to serve as best I can for my whole life.

I love my two brothers, Ronnie and Jeff. Three bros. The best. Special thanks to Ronnie. There's no way I could have published this book, or my first book, *Settle It! . . . and be Blessed*, without him. When helping the family all these years, he always gets it right. Amazing.

And to my friend and publicist, Chris Bridges. Thanks for all your ongoing help. I really enjoy the speeches and events you set up for me. You get it. I just want to help people with the message of this book, which is, *turn your life over to the ultimate problem solver and He will, in deed and in truth, solve your problems and insure eternity for you.* And in the same way, thanks for your help with *Settle It . . . and be Blessed.*

And to my friends, David and Debbie Ashwell. I really appreciate your help on the covers for my books, the encouragement, and the warmth of your friendship. And our mutual friends David Dreier and Brad Smith. Apparently, we all think we still have much to do in this grand life experience. New goals and dreams just keep piling up.

And to my editor, Teri Wilhelms. Thank you, Teri. I couldn't have asked for a better partner in getting my two books so professionally edited.

Thank You, Lord, for all those counseling sessions, and all the wonderful people you put in my path. Looking forward to more of both to come.

Tom Gehring
June 18, 2014

Contact Tom

I would certainly appreciate any thoughts, comments, questions, complaints, or praises you may have and want to share with me about *The Problem Solver*.

If you'd like to contact me, here is the contact information for my law firm:

Tom Gehring
1534 17th Street
Unit 203
Santa Monica, CA 90404
tom@tomgehring.com
310-264-7744

I hope I hear from you.

Tom

Telos.